100 ESSENTIAL

AMERICAN POEMS

Also Edited by Leslie M. Pockell

The 100 Best Poems of All Time

The 100 Best Love Poems of All Time

100 Poems to Lift Your Spirits

100 ESSENTIAL AMERICAN POEMS

Edited by Leslie M. Pockell

THOMAS DUNNE BOOKS

ST. MARTIN'S PRESS 〰 NEW YORK

THOMAS DUNNE BOOKS.
An imprint of St. Martin's Press.

100 ESSENTIAL AMERICAN POEMS. Copyright © 2009 by Leslie M. Pockell. All rights reserved. Printed in the United States of America. For information, address St. Martin's Press, 175 Fifth Avenue, New York, N.Y. 10010.

www.thomasdunnebooks.com
www.stmartins.com

Library of Congress Cataloging-in-Publication Data

100 essential American poems / edited by Leslie M. Pockell.—1st ed.
    p. cm.
  ISBN-13: 978-0-312-36980-4
  ISBN-10: 0-312-36980-8
  1. American poetry.   I. Pockell, Leslie.   II. Title: One hundred essential American poems.
  PS586.A125 2009
  811.008—dc21   2008038641

First Edition: April 2009

10 9 8 7 6 5 4 3 2 1

FOR NORIKO

CONTENTS

Introduction — *xiii*

The Prologue by Anne Bradstreet — 2

The Author to Her Book by Anne Bradstreet — 5

Before the Birth of One of Her Children by Anne Bradstreet — 6

To My Dear and Loving Husband by Anne Bradstreet — 8

Amazing Grace by John Newton — 9

Yankee Doodle Dandy (traditional) — 11

The Star-Spangled Banner by Francis Scott Key — 13

A Visit from St. Nicholas by Clement Clarke Moore — 15

Thanatopsis by William Cullen Bryant — 18

Concord Hymn by Ralph Waldo Emerson — 22

Paul Revere's Ride by Henry Wadsworth Longfellow — 24

The Village Blacksmith by Henry Wadsworth Longfellow — 29

A Psalm of Life by Henry Wadsworth Longfellow — 32

Barbara Frietchie by John Greenleaf Whittier — 34

Snow-Bound by John Greenleaf Whittier — 38

Old Ironsides by Oliver Wendell Holmes   59

The Chambered Nautilus by Oliver Wendell Holmes   62

The Deacon's Masterpiece, or The Wonderful
    "One-Hoss Shay" by Oliver Wendell Holmes   64

The Raven by Edgar Allan Poe   69

To Helen by Edgar Allan Poe   75

The Bells by Edgar Allan Poe   76

What Is So Rare As a Day in June from "The Vision of
    Sir Launfal" by James Russell Lowell   80

Billy in the Darbies by Herman Melville   83

What is the grass from *Leaves of Grass* by Walt Whitman   86

Out of the Cradle Endlessly Rocking by Walt Whitman   88

Crossing Brooklyn Ferry by Walt Whitman   96

A Noiseless Patient Spider by Walt Whitman   104

I Hear America Singing by Walt Whitman   105

When I Heard the Learn'd Astronomer by Walt Whitman   106

When Lilacs Last in the Dooryard Bloom'd by Walt Whitman   107

Battle-Hymn of the Republic by Julia Ward Howe   119

Go Down, Moses (traditional)   121

Follow the Drinking Gourd (traditional)   123

Jeanie with the Light Brown Hair by Stephen C. Foster   125

Old Folks at Home by Stephen C. Foster   127

Wild nights!—wild nights! by Emily Dickinson   130

There is no frigate like a book by Emily Dickinson   131

"Hope" is the thing with feathers by Emily Dickinson   132

I taste a liquor never brewed by Emily Dickinson   133

I'm nobody! Who are you? by Emily Dickinson   134

Because I could not stop for Death by Emily Dickinson   135

The Face on the Barroom Floor by Hugh Antoine D'Arcy   136

Git Along, Little Dogies (traditional)   140

Sioux Ghost Dance (translated by James Mooney)   142

The New Colossus by Emma Lazarus   144

Little Boy Blue by Eugene Field   146

Casey at the Bat by Ernest Thayer   148

Richard Cory by Edwin Arlington Robinson   151

Anne Rutledge from *Spoon River Anthology* by
   Edgar Lee Masters   153

A Man Said to the Universe by Stephen Crane   154

In the Desert (from *The Black Riders and Other Lines*)
   by Stephen Crane   155

The Cremation of Sam McGee by Robert W. Service   156

The Shooting of Dan McGrew by Robert W. Service   161

Lift Every Voice and Sing by James Weldon Johnson   165

We Wear the Mask by Paul Laurence Dunbar   167

The Congo by Vachel Lindsay   168

A Decade by Amy Lowell   177

The Gift Outright by Robert Frost 178

The Road Not Taken by Robert Frost 180

Stopping by Woods on a Snowy Evening by Robert Frost 182

Mending Wall by Robert Frost 183

Death of the Hired Man by Robert Frost 185

Chicago by Carl Sandburg 192

Fog by Carl Sandburg 194

Grass by Carl Sandburg 195

The Emperor of Ice-Cream by Wallace Stevens 196

Thirteen Ways of Looking at a Blackbird by Wallace Stevens 198

Home by Edgar Guest 202

The Red Wheelbarrow by William Carlos Williams 204

This Is Just to Say by William Carlos Williams 205

Ancient Music by Ezra Pound 206

Trees by Joyce Kilmer 207

Poetry by Marianne Moore 209

The Love Song of J. Alfred Prufrock by Thomas
    Stearns Eliot 212

The Waste Land by Thomas Stearns Eliot 219

First Fig by Edna St. Vincent Millay 240

I, Being Born a Woman and Distressed by
    Edna St. Vincent Millay 241

Spring by Edna St. Vincent Millay 242

Recuerdo by Edna St. Vincent Millay 243

Second Fig by Edna St. Vincent Millay 244

Résumé by Dorothy Parker 245

Buffalo Bill's by E. E. Cummings 246

In Just- by E.E. Cummings 247

Proem: To Brooklyn Bridge by Hart Crane 249

Dream Deferred by Langston Hughes 252

Mother to Son by Langston Hughes 254

Song of the Open Road by Ogden Nash 255

Reflections on Ice-breaking by Ogden Nash 256

Cross Roads Blues by Robert Johnson 258

Stagger Lee (traditional) 259

One Art by Elizabeth Bishop 261

This Land Is Your Land by Woody Guthrie 263

The Death of the Ball Turret Gunner by Randall Jarrell 265

For the Union Dead by Robert Lowell 266

We Real Cool by Gwendolyn Brooks 270

Sound Off Marching Cadence Count (derived from
    the Duckworth Chant, originally attributed to
    Pvt. Willie Duckworth) 271

The Day Lady Died by Frank O'Hara 276

A Supermarket in California by Allen Ginsberg   278

Daddy by Sylvia Plath   280

Taking Off Emily Dickinson's Clothes by Billy Collins   284

Permissions   287

INTRODUCTION

The way we view our nation—its history, its traditions, even what we consider our American voice—is largely determined by our literature. In this book I have gathered poems that I feel are essential components of our common American culture. Not that these are the only works of literature that could have been included, but I've limited the number to one hundred for conciseness and because within such a narrow scope influences and commonalities are more easily distinguished. I've organized the poems in a loosely chronological order, based on the poet's year of birth, or the approximate period when the poem first appeared.

Because American culture, taken as a whole, is a mixture of good and bad, and because attitudes, tastes, and styles evolve over time, not all the poems included here are today considered great literary works. But I feel strongly that each of the works included here adds something important, yes, even *essential*, to our understanding of the roots of our shared culture. Some of the poems are essential to the way we look at the history of our country—songs and anthems, poems of praise and patriotic glory. Others act as a kind of corrective to some of our assumptions, such as the Sioux Ghost Dance that helped lead to the massacre at Wounded Knee, or Randall Jarrell's stark war poem "The Death of the Ball Turret Gunner."

Many of the poems here have helped create what most of us consider a fundamentally American tradition: "A Visit from St. Nicholas" and "Casey at the Bat" are examples, and so are sentimental verses like Eugene Field's "Little Boy Blue," Joyce Kilmer's "Trees," and Edgar

Guest's "Home." The figure of Abraham Lincoln appears in a number of the poems included in this collection, but it is not the historical Lincoln, but the legendary and now traditional figure of the martyred president, which has been passed down to us through such works as Whitman's "When Lilacs Last in the Dooryard Bloom'd" and Edgar Lee Masters's "Anne Rutledge."

A great many of these poems are simply classics, foundation blocks of the canon of American literature, from "Thanatopsis" and "The Raven" to "Death of the Hired Hand" and "The Love Song of J. Alfred Prufrock." These are poems that we often first encounter in school, but that become part of the fabric of who we are and how we think about ourselves and the world at large.

A substantial number of these poems, especially those written over the past hundred years, have contributed significantly to what we might consider a characteristic American voice. Of course, the poems did not create that voice, but in attempting to reflect the genuine tone and cadence of everyday conversation, while registering original and sometimes startling poetic images, much of the poetry collected here represents a recognizably American speech, much as Shakespeare, Marlowe, and Ben Jonson preserved the flowering of Elizabethan English. In the very first poet to appear in the book, the Puritan Anne Bradstreet, we can distinguish a singular voice, a woman's voice, that is echoed in some manner down the centuries through Emily Dickinson, Edna St. Vincent Millay, Dorothy Parker, and even Sylvia Plath. The themes of race and slavery form a steady current throughout these poems, almost a dialogue between white voices and black, from the eighteenth-century hymn "Amazing Grace" by the repentant slave trader John Newton, through Negro spirituals, the surprisingly sympathetic "plantation songs" of Stephen Foster, the distorted but powerful rhythms of Vachel Lindsay's "The Congo," the authentic voices of African American poets and lyricists, and even the tortured reflections of Robert Lowell's "For the Union Dead." When Robert Frost presents a conversation between a farmer and his wife, William Carlos Williams leaves a note in the kitchen, and Frank O'Hara recalls a lunchtime excursion, their poems and many more in this book are recording a conversational American English that is at the same time the language of great art.

And finally, what all of these poems in their variety convey is a sensibility that can only be considered essentially American. Sometimes the sensibility is humorous, whether gently exaggerating, as in "The Wonderful One-Hoss Shay," or savagely ironic, as in Dorothy Parker's "Résumé." Sometimes it is grandiose, as in Whitman's all-embracing celebrations or Hart Crane's passionate paean to the symbolic strand of the Brooklyn Bridge. The poems here are filled with patriotic pride, or love of nature, or a sense of alienation from others that we paradoxically share with those around us—these, too, are parts of a national sensibility that is manifestly and uniquely American, if not in their sentiments, then in their manner of expression. The hundred poems and lyrics contained in this book do not encompass all of American tradition and culture, but they evoke them powerfully and provide an entry to a greater understanding of what it means to partake of them, as we all do.

I'd like to thank Tom Dunne, my friend of many years, for suggesting this project. It's given us even more opportunity to discuss life and literature than we've had in the past, and this time with an actual object in view. I'd also like to thank Celia Johnson for her significant editorial contributions.

—LESLIE M. POCKELL
White Plains, New York
June 2008

ANNE BRADSTREET

(1612–1672)

Anne Bradstreet is known as America's first great woman poet, but that reputation is insufficient—she was a great poet who happened to be an American and a woman. She was Puritan through and through, by birth and marriage (she arrived in Salem, Massachusetts, in 1630, with her father and husband), but it's clear from her work that she was a person of independent mind. Any reader of Anne Bradstreet's poetry must be aware of her effort to express herself in an environment with strong assumptions about the appropriateness, or even the possibility, of such expression. Yet perhaps the most significant impression to be drawn from reading her work is its essential modernity—although these words were written well over three centuries ago, we experience them with complete immediacy. It's interesting to compare her tone with that of the twentieth-century poet Edna St. Vincent Millay.

This poem seems to be a proclamation of modesty in the face of male superiority, but it is reasonable to wonder if the words might have been written with at least a touch of irony.

The Prologue

1

To sing of wars, of captains, and of kings,
Of cities founded, common-wealths begun,
For my mean pen, are too superior things;
And how they all, or each, their dates have run
Let poets, and historians set these forth,
My obscure verse shall not so dim their worth.

2

But when my wond'ring eyes, and envious heart,
Great Bartas' sugared lines do but read o'er,
Fool, I do grudge the Muses did not part
'Twixt him and me that over-fluent store;
A Bartas can do what a Bartas will,
But simple I, according to my skill.

3

From school-boys tongue no rhetoric we expect,
Nor yet a sweet consort, from broken strings,
Nor perfect beauty where's a main defect;
My foolish, broken, blemished Muse so sings;
And this to mend, alas, no art is able,
'Cause nature made it so irreparable.

4

Nor can I, like that fluent sweet-tongued Greek
Who lisped at first, speak afterwards more plain.
By art, he gladly found what he did seek,
A full requital of his striving pain:
Art can do much, but this maxim's most sure.
A weak or wounded brain admits no cure.

5

I am obnoxious to each carping tongue,
Who says my hand a needle better fits;
A poet's pen all scorn I should thus wrong;
For such despite they cast on female wits:
If what I do prove well, it won't advance,
They'll say it's stolen, or else it was by chance.

6

But sure the antick Greeks were far more mild,
Else of our sex, why feigned they those nine,
And poesy made Calliope's owne child?
So 'mongst the rest, they placed the arts divine:
But this weak knot they will full soon untie,
The Greeks did nought, but play the fools and lie.

7

Let Greeks be Greeks, and women what they are,
Men have precedency and still excel;
It is but vain, unjustly to wage war;
Men can do best, and women know it well;
Preeminence in each and all is yours,
Yet grant some small acknowledgment of ours.

8

And oh, ye high flown quills that soar the skies,
And ever with your prey, still catch your praise,
If e'er you deign these lowly lines your eyes,
Give wholesome parsley wreath, I ask no bays:
This mean and unrefinèd ore of mine,
Will make your glistering gold but more to shine.

Here the poem is compared to the poet's child, not perfect, but beloved all the same.

The Author to Her Book

Thou ill-formed offspring of my feeble brain,
Who after birth didst by my side remain,
Till snatched from thence by friends, less wise than true,
Who thee abroad, exposed to public view,
Made thee in rags, halting to th' press to trudge,
Where errors were not lessened (all may judge).
At thy return my blushing was not small,
My rambling brat (in print) should mother call.
I cast thee by as one unfit for light,
The visage was so irksome in my sight;
Yet being mine own, at length affection would
Thy blemishes amend, if so I could.
I washed thy face, but more defects I saw,
And rubbing off a spot, still made a flaw.
I stretched thy joints to make thee even feet,
Yet still thou run'st more hobbling than is meet;
In better dress to trim thee was my mind,
But nought save home-spun cloth, i' th' house I find.
In this array, 'mongst vulgars may'st thou roam.
In critic's hands, beware thou dost not come,
And take thy way where yet thou art not known;
If for thy father asked, say thou hadst none;
And for thy mother, she alas is poor,
Which caused her thus to send thee out of door.

Death in or soon after childbirth was so commom in Colonial days, it is
not surprising, though still a little heartbreaking, that the poet felt the
need to compose a kind of farewell to her child even before it was born.

Before the Birth of One of Her Children

All things within this fading world hath end,
Adversity doth still our joys attend;
No ties so strong, no friends so dear and sweet,
But with death's parting blow are sure to meet.
The sentence past is most irrevocable,
A common thing, yet oh inevitable;
How soon, my dear, death may my steps attend,
How soon't may be thy lot to lose thy friend;
We both are ignorant, yet love bids me
These farewell lines to recommend to thee,
That when the knot's untied that made us one,
I may seem thine, who in effect am none.
And if I see not half my days that's due,
What nature would, God grant to yours and you;
The many faults that well you know I have,
Let be interr'd in my oblivion's grave;
If any worth or virtue were in me,
Let that live freshly in thy memory,
And when thou feel'st no grief, as I no harms,
Yet love thy dead, who long lay in thine arms:
And when thy loss shall be repaid with gains,
Look to my little babes, my dear remains.
And if thou love thy self, or loved'st me,

These O protect from step-dame's injury.
And if chance to thine eyes shall bring this verse,
With some sad sighs honor my absent Hearse;
And kiss this paper for thy dear love's sake,
Who with salt tears this last farewell did take.

This tribute to a marriage conveys a complexity and passion quite different from the usual image of American Puritans.

To My Dear and Loving Husband

If ever two were one, then surely we.
If ever man were loved by wife, then thee;
If ever wife was happy in a man,
Compare with me ye women if you can.
I prize thy love more than whole mines of gold,
Or all the riches that the East doth hold.
My love is such that rivers cannot quench,
Nor ought but love from thee give recompense.
Thy love is such I can no way repay;
The heavens reward thee manifold, I pray.
Then while we live, in love let's so persever,
That when we live no more we may live ever.

JOHN NEWTON
(1725–1807)

John Newton was the captain of a slave ship when, in 1748, he experienced what he later called a "great deliverance" during a powerful storm at sea. He later gave up sailing and became a Methodist minister and writer of hymns, collaborating with the eminent English poet William Cowper. Ironically, the melody to which these verses are now sung quite possibly was originally sung by African slaves in America.

Amazing Grace

Amazing grace! How sweet the sound
That sav'd a wretch like me!
I once was lost, but now am found,
Was blind, but now I see.

'Twas grace that taught my heart to fear,
And grace my fears reliev'd;
How precious did that grace appear
The hour I first believ'd!

Thro' many dangers, toils and snares
I have already come;
'Tis grace hath brought me safe thus far;
And grace will lead me home.

The Lord has promis'd good to me,
His word my hope secures;
He will my shield and portion be
As long as life endures.

Yes, when this flesh and heart shall fail,
And mortal life shall cease;
I shall possess, within the veil,
A life of joy and peace.

The earth shall soon dissolve like snow,
The sun forbear to shine;
But God, who call'd me here below,
Will be forever mine.

TRADITIONAL

(CA. 1775)

A version of this most quintessentially American of all American folk songs was originally sung by British soldiers mocking the ragtag look of American militiamen during the French and Indian War. Supposedly a troop of soldiers from Norwalk, Connecticut, commanded by Thomas Fitch, wore civilian clothes, but each trooper displayed a feather in his cap in a small effort at creating a uniform look. The song changed sides at the time of the American Revolution, and new verses were added reflecting this. It is said that American soldiers at the Battle of Bunker Hill played the tune back at the British soldiers, one of whom was later quoted as saying "they made us dance to it till we were tired!"

Yankee Doodle Dandy

Yankee Doodle went to town
A-riding on a pony
Stuck a feather in his hat
And called it macaroni.

Yankee Doodle, keep it up
Yankee Doodle dandy
Mind the music and the step
And with the girls be handy.

Father and I went down to camp
Along with Captain Gooding
And there we saw the men and boys
As thick as hasty pudding.

Yankee Doodle, keep it up
Yankee Doodle dandy
Mind the music and the step
And with the girls be handy.

There was Captain Washington
Upon a slapping stallion
A-giving orders to his men
I guess there was a million.

Yankee Doodle, keep it up
Yankee Doodle dandy
Mind the music and the step
And with the girls be handy.

FRANCIS SCOTT KEY
(1779–1843)

In 1814, during the War of 1812, part of the British fleet attacked Fort McHenry in Baltimore Harbor in an attempt to seize the city. Francis Scott Key, a prominent attorney, watched the battle from a ship in the harbor behind British lines. From his vantage point he and his companions could make out the flag flying from the fort's walls, but as the battle continued through the night, he could only catch occasional glimpses of it in flashes from the British bombardment. Firing ceased before dawn, but only after the sun rose was Key able to see that the flag of the United States still flew atop the fort. Originally entitled the "Defence of Fort McHenry," Key's verses written that morning, sung to the tune of a popular drinking song, soon became known by the title familiar to us today, but it only became the official national anthem of the United States of America in 1931.

The Star-Spangled Banner

O! say can you see, by the dawn's early light,
  What so proudly we hail'd at the twilight's last gleaming,
Whose broad stripes and bright stars through the perilous fight, ·
    O'er the ramparts we watch'd, were so gallantly streaming?
      And the rockets' red glare, the bombs bursting in air,
        Gave proof through the night that our flag was still there—
          O! say, does that star-spangled banner yet wave
          O'er the land of the free and the home of the brave?

On the shore, dimly seen through the mists of the deep,
  Where the foe's haughty host in dread silence reposes,
What is that which the breeze, o'er the towering steep,
  As it fitfully blows, half conceals, half discloses?
    Now it catches the gleam of the morning's first beam,
    In full glory reflected, now shines on the stream—
      'Tis the star-spangled banner, O! long may it wave
      O'er the land of the free and the home of the brave.

And where is that band who so vauntingly swore
  That the havock of war and the battle's confusion
A home and a country should leave us no more?
  Their blood has wash'd out their foul foot-steps' pollution.
    No refuge could save the hireling and slave,
    From the terror of flight or the gloom of the grave;
      And the star-spangled banner in triumph doth wave
      O'er the land of the free and the home of the brave.

O! thus be it ever when freemen shall stand
  Between their lov'd home, and the war's desolation,
Blest with vict'ry and peace, may the heav'n-rescued land
  Praise the power that hath made and preserv'd us as a nation!
    Then conquer we must, when our cause is just,
    And this be our motto—"In God is our trust!"
      And the star-spangled banner in triumph shall wave
      O'er the land of the free, and the home of the brave.

CLEMENT CLARKE MOORE
(1779–1863)

Clement Clarke Moore was a wealthy New York scholar (he grew up on an estate that is today known as the Chelsea section of Manhattan) who is remembered as the author of "A Visit from St. Nicholas," not only an immensely popular poem in its own right, but one that created an idealized image of the celebration of Christmas in America that extends to this day. The poem was published anonymously in a Troy, New York, newspaper in 1822, and Moore did not claim credit for it until years later, which has led to some speculation as to whether this professorial figure was in fact the author of such a folksy classic.

A Visit from St. Nicholas

'Twas the night before Christmas, when all through the house
Not a creature was stirring, not even a mouse;
The stockings were hung by the chimney with care,
In hopes that St. Nicholas soon would be there;
The children were nestled all snug in their beds,
While visions of sugar plums danced in their heads;
And mamma in her 'kerchief, and I in my cap,
Had just settled down for a long winter's nap,
When out on the lawn there arose such a clatter,
I sprang from the bed to see what was the matter.
Away to the window I flew like a flash,
Tore open the shutters and threw up the sash.
The moon on the breast of the new-fallen snow
Gave the luster of midday to objects below,

When, what to my wondering eyes should appear,
But a miniature sleigh, and eight tiny reindeer,
With a little old driver, so lively and quick,
I knew in a moment it must be St. Nick.
More rapid than eagles his coursers they came,
And he whistled, and shouted, and called them by name;
"Now, *Dasher!* now, *Dancer!* Now, *Prancer* and *Vixen!*
On, *Comet!* On *Cupid!* On, *Donder* and *Blitzen!*
To the top of the porch! to the top of the wall!
Now dash away! dash away! dash away all!"
As dry leaves that before the wild hurricane fly,
When they meet with an obstacle, mount to the sky;
So up to the house top the coursers they flew,
With the sleigh full of toys, and St. Nicholas, too.
And then, in a twinkling, I heard on the roof
The prancing and pawing of each little hoof.
As I drew in my head, and was turning around,
Down the chimney St. Nicholas came with a bound.
He was dressed all in fur, from his head to his foot,
And his clothes were all tarnished with ashes and soot;
A bundle of toys he had flung on his back,
And he looked like a peddler just opening his pack.
His eyes—how they twinkled! His dimples how merry!
His cheeks were like roses, his nose like a cherry!
His droll little mouth was drawn up like a bow,
And the beard of his chin was as white as the snow;
The stump of a pipe he held tight in his teeth,
And the smoke it encircled his head like a wreath;
He had a broad face and a little round belly,
That shook when he laughed like a bowlful of jelly.
He was chubby and plump, a right jolly old elf,
And I laughed when I saw him, in spite of myself;
A wink of his eye and a twist of his head,

Soon gave me to know I had nothing to dread;
He spoke not a word, but went straight to his work,
And filled all the stockings; then turned with a jerk,
And laying his finger aside of his nose,
And giving a nod, up the chimney he rose;
He sprang to his sleigh, to his team gave a whistle,
And away they all flew like the down of a thistle.
But I heard him exclaim, ere he drove out of sight,
"Happy Christmas to all, and to all a good night!"

WILLIAM CULLEN BRYANT
(1794–1878)

William Cullen Bryant was a child prodigy who wrote the momentous poem below while still in his teens. The title is an invented Greek word meaning "Viewing Death," and it is almost startling to think that the philosophical and pantheistic view of existence expressed here emerged from someone in his late adolescence. At the same time, it is worth remembering that Bryant was an exact contemporary of Keats, Shelley, and Byron, and with this poem was in effect establishing a branch of the British romantic tradition in America. Bryant went on to become an eminent journalist active in the antislavery movement; Bryant Park in New York City is named for him.

Thanatopsis

To him who in the love of Nature holds
Communion with her visible forms, she speaks
A various language; for his gayer hours
She has a voice of gladness, and a smile
And eloquence of beauty, and she glides
Into his darker musings, with a mild
And healing sympathy, that steals away
Their sharpness, ere he is aware. When thoughts
Of the last bitter hour come like a blight
Over thy spirit, and sad images
Of the stern agony, and shroud, and pall,
And breathless darkness, and the narrow house,
Make thee to shudder, and grow sick at heart;—

Go forth, under the open sky, and list
To Nature's teachings, while from all around—
Earth and her waters, and the depths of air—
Comes a still voice.—

                      Yet a few days, and thee
The all-beholding sun shall see no more
In all his course; nor yet in the cold ground,
Where thy pale form was laid, with many tears,
Nor in the embrace of ocean, shall exist
Thy image. Earth, that nourished thee, shall claim
Thy growth, to be resolved to earth again,
And, lost each human trace, surrendering up
Thine individual being, shalt thou go
To mix for ever with the elements,
To be a brother to the insensible rock
And to the sluggish clod, which the rude swain
Turns with his share, and treads upon. The oak
Shall send his roots abroad, and pierce thy mould.

  Yet not to thine eternal resting-place
Shalt thou retire alone, nor couldst thou wish
Couch more magnificent. Thou shalt lie down
With patriarchs of the infant world—with kings,
The powerful of the earth—the wise, the good,
Fair forms, and hoary seers of ages past,
All in one mighty sepulchre. The hills
Rock-ribbed and ancient as the sun,—the vales
Stretching in pensive quietness between;
The venerable woods—rivers that move
In majesty, and the complaining brooks
That make the meadows green; and, poured round all,
Old Ocean's gray and melancholy waste,—
Are but the solemn decorations all

Of the great tomb of man. The golden sun,
The planets, all the infinite host of heaven,
Are shining on the sad abodes of death,
Through the still lapse of ages. All that tread
The globe are but a handful to the tribes
That slumber in its bosom.—Take the wings
Of morning, pierce the Barcan wilderness,
Or lose thyself in the continuous woods
Where rolls the Oregon and hears no sound,
Save his own dashings—yet the dead are there:
And millions in those solitudes, since first
The flight of years began, have laid them down
In their last sleep—the dead reign there alone.
So shalt thou rest, and what if thou withdraw
In silence from the living, and no friend
Take note of thy departure? All that breathe
Will share thy destiny. The gay will laugh
When thou art gone, the solemn brood of care
Plod on, and each one as before will chase
His favorite phantom; yet all these shall leave
Their mirth and their employments, and shall come
And make their bed with thee. As the long train
Of ages glides away, the sons of men,
The youth in life's green spring, and he who goes
In the full strength of years, matron and maid,
The speechless babe, and the gray-headed man—
Shall one by one be gathered to thy side,
By those, who in their turn shall follow them.

So live, that when thy summons comes to join
The innumerable caravan, which moves
To that mysterious realm, where each shall take
His chamber in the silent halls of death,
Thou go not, like the quarry-slave at night,
Scourged by his dungeon, but, sustained and soothed
By an unfaltering trust, approach thy grave,
Like one who wraps the drapery of his couch
About him, and lies down to pleasant dreams.

RALPH WALDO EMERSON
(1803–1882)

This poem was written to mark the dedication of a monument near the old North Bridge, the site of the Battle of Concord on April 19, 1775, in which British regulars were turned back by members of the Colonial militia (called Minutemen because of their ability to assemble at short notice). The dedication was originally scheduled for April 19, 1836, but it was delayed until July 4 of the following year. Visitors to the site will find on the other side of the now reconstructed bridge a statue of a Minuteman, standing by his plow and holding a musket. The statue, by Daniel Chester French, was placed there in 1875 to mark the centennial of the battle.

Concord Hymn

By the rude bridge that arched the flood,
Their flag to April's breeze unfurled,
Here once the embattled farmers stood
And fired the shot heard round the world.

The foe long since in silence slept;
Alike the conqueror silent sleeps;
And Time the ruined bridge has swept
Down the dark stream which seaward creeps.

On this green bank, by this soft stream,
We set to-day a votive stone;
That memory may their deed redeem,
When, like our sires, our sons are gone.

Spirit, that made those heroes dare
To die, or leave their children free,
Bid Time and Nature gently spare
The shaft we raise to them and thee.

HENRY WADSWORTH LONGFELLOW
(1807–1882)

The poem below is part of the mythology of the American Revolution; the Minutemen celebrated in the previous poem by Emerson were supposedly alerted to the imminent arrival of the British soldiers by the warning given by the Boston silversmith Paul Revere. While the poem is not a model of historical accuracy—Revere was not the only rider alerting the populace that night—he was a notable and active patriot (earlier he had created a rather inaccurate and inflammatory engraving of the *Boston Massacre*). The poem was written in 1860, as the United States was moving toward civil war, and it certainly evoked the nation's, and especially New England's, patriotic tradition.

Paul Revere's Ride

Listen, my children and you shall hear
Of the midnight ride of Paul Revere,
On the eighteenth of April, in Seventy-five;
Hardly a man is now alive
Who remembers that famous day and year.

He said to his friend, "If the British march
By land or sea from the town to-night,
Hang a lantern aloft in the belfry arch
Of the North Church tower as a signal light,—
One, if by land, and two, if by sea;
And I on the opposite shore will be,

Ready to ride and spread the alarm
Through every Middlesex village and farm,
For the country folk to be up and to arm."

Then he said "Good-night!" and with muffled oar
Silently rowed to the Charlestown shore,
Just as the moon rose over the bay,
Where swinging wide at her moorings lay
The Somerset, British man-of-war;
A phantom ship, with each mast and spar
Across the moon like a prison bar,
And a huge black hulk, that was magnified
By its own reflection in the tide.

Meanwhile, his friend, through alley and street,
Wanders and watches, with eager ears,
Till in silence around him he hears
The muster of men at the barrack door,
The sound of arms, and the tramp of feet,
And the measured tread of the grenadiers,
Marching down to their boats on the shore.

Then he climbed to the tower of the church,
Up the wooden stairs, with stealthy tread,
To the belfry-chamber overhead,
And startled the pigeons from their perch
On the sombre rafters, that round him made
Masses and moving shapes of shade—
Up the trembling ladder, steep and tall,
To the highest window in the wall,
Where he paused to listen and look down
A moment on the roofs of the town
And the moonlight flowing over all.

Beneath, in the churchyard, lay the dead,
In their night-encampment on the hill,
Wrapped in silence so deep and still
That he could hear, like a sentinel's tread,
The watchful night-wind, as it went
Creeping along from tent to tent,
And seeming to whisper, "All is well!"
A moment only he feels the spell
Of the place and the hour, and the secret dread
Of the lonely belfry and the dead;
For suddenly all his thoughts are bent
On a shadowy something far away,
Where the river widens to meet the bay,—
A line of black that bends and floats
On the rising tide like a bridge of boats.

Meanwhile, impatient to mount and ride,
Booted and spurred, with a heavy stride
On the opposite shore walked Paul Revere.
Now he patted his horse's side,
Now gazed at the landscape far and near,
Then, impetuous, stamped the earth,
And turned and tightened his saddle-girth;
But mostly he watched with eager search
The belfry-tower of the Old North Church,

As it rose above the graves on the hill,
Lonely and spectral and sombre and still.
And lo! as he looks, on the belfry's height
A glimmer, and then a gleam of light!
He springs to the saddle, the bridle he turns,
But lingers and gazes, till full on his sight
A second lamp in the belfry burns!

A hurry of hoofs in a village street,
A shape in the moonlight, a bulk in the dark,
And beneath, from the pebbles, in passing, a spark
Struck out by a steed flying fearless and fleet;
That was all! And yet, through the gloom and the light,
The fate of a nation was riding that night;
And the spark struck out by that steed, in his flight,
Kindled the land into flame with its heat.

He has left the village and mounted the steep,
And beneath him, tranquil and broad and deep,
Is the Mystic, meeting the ocean tides;
And under the alders that skirt its edge,
Now soft on the sand, now loud on the ledge,
Is heard the tramp of his steed as he rides.

It was twelve by the village clock
When he crossed the bridge into Medford town.
He heard the crowing of the cock,
And the barking of the farmer's dog,
And felt the damp of the river fog,
That rises after the sun goes down.

It was one by the village clock,
When he galloped into Lexington
He saw the gilded weathercock
Swim in the moonlight as he passed,
And the meeting-house windows, black and bare,
Gaze at him with a spectral glare,
As if they already stood aghast
At the bloody work they would look upon.

It was two by the village clock,
When he came to the bridge in Concord town.
He heard the bleating of the flock,
And the twitter of birds among the trees,
And felt the breath of the morning breeze
Blowing over the meadow brown.
And one was safe and asleep in his bed
Who at the bridge would be first to fall,
Who that day would be lying dead,
Pierced by a British musket-ball.

You know the rest. In the books you have read,
How the British Regulars fired and fled,—
How the farmers gave them ball for ball,
From behind each fence and farmyard wall,
Chasing the red-coats down the lane,
Then crossing the fields to emerge again
Under the trees at the turn of the road,
And only pausing to fire and load.

So through the night rode Paul Revere;
And so through the night went his cry of alarm
To every Middlesex village and farm,—
A cry of defiance and not of fear,
A voice in the darkness, a knock at the door,
And a word that shall echo forevermore!
For, borne on the night-wind of the Past,
Through all our history, to the last,
In the hour of darkness and peril and need,
The people will waken and listen to hear
The hurrying hoof-beats of that steed,
And the midnight message of Paul Revere.

Longfellow had an international reputation (he is the only American en-shrined in Westminster Abbey's Poets' Corner), but he was a genuinely American poet in more ways than one. He often chose subjects from American history for his major poems, such as *Evangeline* and *The Song of Hiawatha*, amplifying existing legends and developing them to the point where they seemed to be an almost inherent part of the national tradition. In "The Village Blacksmith" he writes of an idealized member of society making his living by the literal sweat of his brow. An undeniable strain of sentimentality runs through the poem, but this, too, is part of the American tradition. Perhaps more to the point, Longfellow wrote this as the railroad was beginning to revolutionize transportation, and the mech-anization of labor was beginning to make inroads on a way of life that had existed for centuries. So to some extent, this celebration of the soul of American labor is also a kind of elegy.

The Village Blacksmith

Under a spreading chestnut tree
  The village smithy stands;
The smith, a mighty man is he,
  With large and sinewy hands;
And the muscles of his brawny arms
  Are strong as iron bands.

His hair is crisp, and black, and long,
    His face is like the tan;
His brow is wet with honest sweat,
    He earns whate'er he can,
And looks the whole world in the face,
    For he owes not any man.

Week in, week out, from morn till night,
    You can hear his bellows blow;
You can hear him swing his heavy sledge,
    With measured beat and slow,
Like a sexton ringing the village bell,
    When the evening sun is low.

And children coming home from school
    Look in at the open door;
They love to see the flaming forge,
    And hear the bellows roar,
And catch the burning sparks that fly
    Like chaff from a threshing floor.

He goes on Sunday to the church,
    And sits among his boys;
He hears the parson pray and preach,
    He hears his daughter's voice,
Singing in the village choir,
    And it makes his heart rejoice.

It sounds to him like her mother's voice,
   Singing in Paradise!
He needs must think of her once more,
   How in the grave she lies;
And with his hard, rough hand he wipes
   A tear out of his eyes.

Toiling,—rejoicing,—sorrowing,
   Onward through life he goes;
Each morning sees some task begin,
   Each evening sees it close;
Something attempted, something done,
   Has earned a night's repose.

Thanks, thanks to thee, my worthy friend,
   For the lesson thou hast taught!
Thus at the flaming forge of life
   Our fortunes must be wrought;
Thus on its sounding anvil shaped
   Each burning deed and thought!

The poem below, first published in 1838, is a call not to arms, but to work toward a greater good. It recalls another Longfellow poem written a few years later, "Excelsior," about a youth climbing a mountain. Both poems seem to express an American philosophy of progress gained by ceaseless labor, one which helped inspire the westward movement of pioneers for much of the rest of the century.

A Psalm of Life

WHAT THE HEART OF THE YOUNG MAN SAID TO THE PSALMIST

Tell me not in mournful numbers,
　"Life is but an empty dream!"
For the soul is dead that slumbers,
　And things are not what they seem.

Life is real! Life is earnest!
　And the grave is not its goal;
"Dust thou art, to dust returnest,"
　Was not spoken of the soul.

Not enjoyment, and not sorrow,
　Is our destined end or way;
But to act, that each to-morrow
　Find us further than to-day.

Art is long, and Time is fleeting,
    And our hearts, though stout and brave,
Still, like muffled drums, are beating
    Funeral marches to the grave.

In the world's broad field of battle,
    In the bivouac of Life,
Be not like dumb, driven cattle!
    Be a hero in the strife!

Trust no Future, howe'er pleasant!
    Let the dead Past bury its dead!
Act,—act in the living Present!
    Heart within, and God o'erhead!

Lives of great men all remind us
    We can make our lives sublime,
And, departing, leave behind us
    Footprints on the sands of time;

Footprints, that perhaps another,
    Sailing o'er life's solemn main,
A forlorn and shipwrecked brother,
    Seeing, shall take heart again.

Let us, then, be up and doing,
    With a heart for any fate;
Still achieving, still pursuing,
    Learn to labor and to wait.

The real story behind "Barbara Frietchie" is almost certainly less colorful than that told in the poem—the historic Barbara Frietchie, ninety-six at the time, did wave her flag out a window at passing troops, but they were Union troops, who applauded the aged patriot. Some weeks before, another patriotic woman had waved the American flag at Stonewall Jackson's victorious soldiers on their way out of town, but evidently this provocative gesture occurred without incident. Somehow reports of these events became combined, in the way of folklore, to make a better story, and a memorable poem.

Barbara Frietchie

Up from the meadows rich with corn,
Clear in the cool September morn,

The clustered spires of Frederick stand
Green-walled by the hills of Maryland.

Round about them orchards sweep,
Apple and peach tree fruited deep,

Fair as the garden of the Lord
To the eyes of the famished rebel horde,

On that pleasant morn of the early fall
When Lee marched over the mountain-wall;

Over the mountains winding down,
Horse and foot, into Frederick town.

Forty flags with their silver stars,
Forty flags with their crimson bars,

Flapped in the morning wind: the sun
Of noon looked down, and saw not one.

Up rose old Barbara Frietchie then,
Bowed with her fourscore years and ten;

Bravest of all in Frederick town,
She took up the flag the men hauled down

In her attic window the staff she set,
To show that one heart was loyal yet.

Up the street came the rebel tread,
Stonewall Jackson riding ahead.

Under his slouched hat left and right
He glanced; the old flag met his sight.

"Halt!"—the dust-brown ranks stood fast.
"Fire!"—out blazed the rifle-blast.

It shivered the window, pane and sash;
It rent the banner with seam and gash.

Quick, as it fell, from the broken staff
Dame Barbara snatched the silken scarf.

She leaned far out on the window-sill,
And shook it forth with a royal will.

"Shoot, if you must, this old gray head,
But spare your country's flag," she said.

A shade of sadness, a blush of shame,
Over the face of the leader came;

The nobler nature within him stirred
To life at that woman's deed and word;

"Who touches a hair of yon gray head
Dies like a dog! March on!" he said.

All day long through Frederick street
Sounded the tread of marching feet:

All day long that free flag tost
Over the heads of the rebel host.

Ever its torn folds rose and fell
On the loyal winds that loved it well;

And through the hill-gaps sunset light
Shone over it with a warm good-night.

Barbara Frietchie's work is o'er,
And the rebel rides on his raids no more.

Honor to her! and let a tear
Fall, for her sake, on Stonewall's bier.

Over Barbara Frietchie's grave,
Flag of Freedom and Union, wave!

Peace and order and beauty draw
Round thy symbol of light and law;

And ever the stars above look down
On thy stars below in Frederick town!

Whittier's masterwork was an attempt to preserve the image of a way of life that was vanishing even at the time of the poem's enormously successful publication in 1866. To read the poem today is to receive a surprisingly vivid copy of that image, one only superficially familiar to us from Currier & Ives prints and a kind of archetypal memory that the poem itself helped to create. The very specificity of the descriptions of people, places, and contemporary events makes the poem almost a document of social history as well as a memorable poetic experience (the individuals described in the poem were members of the Whittier family: father, mother, brother, sisters, unmarried uncle and aunt, as well as the district schoolmaster who boarded with the family). The version below is slightly abridged—some of the poem's references are too obscure for most of today's readers—but it still has the scope and breadth of a sort of domestic epic, one that helped form an idealized vision of rural America that persists to this day.

Snow-Bound
A Winter Idyl

TO THE MEMORY OF THE HOUSEHOLD IT DESCRIBES
THIS POEM IS DEDICATED BY THE AUTHOR

As the Spirits of Darkness be stronger in the dark, so Good Spirits, which be Angels of Light, are augmented not only by the Divine light of the Sun, but also by our common Wood Fire: and as the Celestial Fire drives away dark spirits, so also this our Fire of Wood doth the same.

COR. AGRIPPA, *Occult Philosophy*, Book I, ch. v.

Announced by all the trumpets of the sky,
Arrives the snow, and, driving o'er the fields,
Seems nowhere to alight: the whited air
Hides hills and woods, the river and the heaven,
And veils the farm-house at the garden's end.
The sled and traveller stopped, the courier's feet
Delayed, all friends shut out, the housemates sit
Around the radiant fireplace, enclosed
In a tumultuous privacy of Storm.

EMERSON. "The Snow Storm"

The sun that brief December day
Rose cheerless over hills of gray,
And, darkly circled, gave at noon
A sadder light than waning moon.
Slow tracing down the thickening sky
Its mute and ominous prophecy,
A portent seeming less than threat,
It sank from sight before it set.
A chill no coat, however stout,
Of homespun stuff could quite shut out,
A hard, dull bitterness of cold,
That checked, mid-vein, the circling race
Of life-blood in the sharpened face,
The coming of the snow-storm told.
The wind blew east; we heard the roar
Of Ocean on his wintry shore,
And felt the strong pulse throbbing there
Beat with low rhythm our inland air.

Meanwhile we did our nightly chores,—
Brought in the wood from out of doors,
Littered the stalls, and from the mows
Raked down the herd's-grass for the cows:
Heard the horse whinnying for his corn;
And, sharply clashing horn on horn,
Impatient down the stanchion rows
The cattle shake their walnut bows;
While, peering from his early perch
Upon the scaffold's pole of birch,
The cock his crested helmet bent
And down his querulous challenge sent.

Unwarmed by any sunset light
The gray day darkened into night,
A night made hoary with the swarm
And whirl-dance of the blinding storm,
As zigzag, wavering to and fro,
Crossed and recrossed the wingèd snow:
And ere the early bedtime came
The white drift piled the window-frame,
And through the glass the clothes-line posts
Looked in like tall and sheeted ghosts.

*   *   *   *   *

The old familiar sights of ours
Took marvellous shapes; strange domes and towers
Rose up where sty or corn-crib stood,
Or garden-wall, or belt of wood;
A smooth white mound the brush-pile showed,
A fenceless drift what once was road;
The bridle-post an old man sat
With loose-flung coat and high cocked hat;

The well-curb had a Chinese roof;
And even the long sweep, high aloof,
In its slant spendor, seemed to tell
Of Pisa's leaning miracle.

A prompt, decisive man, no breath
Our father wasted: "Boys, a path!"
Well pleased, (for when did farmer boy
Count such a summons less than joy?)
Our buskins on our feet we drew;
With mittened hands, and caps drawn low,
To guard our necks and ears from snow,
We cut the solid whiteness through.
And, where the drift was deepest, made
A tunnel walled and overlaid
With dazzling crystal: we had read
Of rare Aladdin's wondrous cave,
And to our own his name we gave,
With many a wish the luck were ours
To test his lamp's supernal powers.
We reached the barn with merry din,
And roused the prisoned brutes within.
The old horse thrust his long head out,
And grave with wonder gazed about;
The cock his lusty greeting said,
And forth his speckled harem led;
The oxen lashed their tails, and hooked,
And mild reproach of hunger looked;
The hornëd patriarch of the sheep,
Like Egypt's Amun roused from sleep,
Shook his sage head with gesture mute,
And emphasized with stamp of foot.

All day the gusty north-wind bore
The loosening drift its breath before;
Low circling round its southern zone,
The sun through dazzling snow-mist shone.
No church-bell lent its Christian tone
To the savage air, no social smoke
Curled over woods of snow-hung oak.
A solitude made more intense
By dreary-voicëd elements,
The shrieking of the mindless wind,
The moaning tree-boughs swaying blind,
And on the glass the unmeaning beat
Of ghostly finger-tips of sleet.
Beyond the circle of our hearth
No welcome sound of toil or mirth
Unbound the spell, and testified
Of human life and thought outside.
We minded that the sharpest ear
The buried brooklet could not hear,
The music of whose liquid lip
Had been to us companionship,
And, in our lonely life, had grown
To have an almost human tone.

As night drew on, and, from the crest
Of wooded knolls that ridged the west,
The sun, a snow-blown traveller, sank
From sight beneath the smothering bank,
We piled, with care, our nightly stack
Of wood against the chimney-back,—
The oaken log, green, huge, and thick,
And on its top the stout back-stick;
The knotty forestick laid apart,

And filled between with curious art
The ragged brush; then, hovering near,
We watched the first red blaze appear,
Heard the sharp crackle, caught the gleam
On whitewashed wall and sagging beam,
Until the old, rude-furnished room
Burst, flower-like, into rosy bloom;
While radiant with a mimic flame
Outside the sparkling drift became,
And through the bare-boughed lilac-tree
Our own warm hearth seemed blazing free,
The crane and pendent trammels showed,
The Turks' heads on the andirons glowed;
While childish fancy, prompt to tell
The meaning of the miracle,
Whispered the old rhyme: *"Under the tree,*
When fire outdoors burns merrily,
There the witches are making tea."

The moon above the eastern wood
Shone at its full; the hill-range stood
Transfigured in the silver flood,
Its blown snows flashing cold and keen,
Dead white, save where some sharp ravine
Took shadow, or the sombre green
Of hemlocks turned to pitchy black
Against the whiteness at their back.
For such a world and such a night
Most fitting that unwarming light,
Which only seemd where'er it fell
To make the coldness visible.

Shut in from all the world without,
We sat the clean-winged hearth about,
Content to let the north-wind roar
In baffled rage at pane and door,
While the red logs before us beat
The frost-line back with tropic heat;
And ever, when a louder blast
Shook beam and rafter as it passed,
The merrier up its roaring draught
The great throat of the chimney laughed;
The house-dog on his paws outspread
Laid to the fire his drowsy head,
The cat's dark silhouette on the wall
A couchant tiger's seemed to fall;
And, for the winter fireside meet,
Between the andirons' straddling feet,
The mug of cider simmered slow,
The apples sputtered in a row,
And, close at hand, the basket stood
With nuts from brown October's wood.

What matter how the night behaved?
What matter how the north-wind raved?
Blow high, blow low, not all its snow
Could quench our hearth-fire's ruddy glow.
O Time and Change!—with hair as gray
As was my sire's that winter day,
How strange it seems, with so much gone
Of life and love, to still live on!
Ah, brother! only I and thou
Are left of all that circle now,—
The dear home faces whereupon
That fitful firelight paled and shone.

Henceforward, listen as we will,
The voices of that hearth are still;
Look where we may, the wide earth o'er,
Those lighted faces smile no more.
We tread the paths their feet have worn,
  We sit beneath their orchard trees,
  We hear, like them, the hum of bees
And rustle of the bladed corn;
We turn the pages that they read,
  Their written words we linger o'er.
But in the sun they cast no shade,
No voice is heard, no sign is made,
  No step is on the conscious floor!
Yet love will dream, and Faith will trust,
(Since He who knows our need is just),
That somehow, somewhere, meet we must.
Alas for him who never sees
The stars shine through his cypress-trees!
Who, hopeless, lays his dead away,
Nor looks to see the breaking day
Across the mournful marbles play!
Who hath not learned, in hours of faith,
  The truth to flesh and sense unknown,
That Life is ever lord of Death,
  And Love can never lose its own!

*   *   *   *   *

Our mother, while she turned her wheel
Or run the new-knit stocking-heel,
Told how the Indian hordes came down
At midnight on Cocheco town,
And how her own great-uncle bore
His cruel scalp-mark to fourscore.

Recalling, in her fitting phrase,
   So rich and picturesque and free,
   (The common unrhymed poetry
Of simple life and country ways),
The story of her early days,—
She made us welcome to her home;
Old hearths grew wide to give us room;
We stole with her a frightened look
At the gray wizard's conjuring-book,
The fame whereof went far and wide
Through all the simple country side;
We heard the hawks at twilight play,
The boat-horn on Piscataqua,
The loon's weird laughter far away;
We fished her little trout-brook, knew
What flowers in wood and meadow grew,
What sunny hillsides autumn-brown
She climbed to shake the ripe nuts down,
Saw where in sheltered cove and bay
The ducks' black squadron anchored lay,
And heard the wild-geese calling loud
Beneath the gray November cloud.

Then, haply, with a look more grave,
And soberer tone, some tale she gave
From painful Sewel's ancient tome,
Beloved in every Quaker home,
Of faith fire-winged by martyrdom,
Or Chalkley's Journal, old and quaint,—
Gentlest of skippers, rare sea-saint!—
Who, when the dreary calms prevailed,
And water-butt and bread-cask failed,
And cruel, hungry eyes pursued

His portly presence mad for food,
With dark hints muttered under breath
Of casting lots for life or death,
Offered, if Heaven withheld supplies,
To be himself the sacrifice.
Then, suddenly, as if to save
The good man from his living grave,
A ripple on the water grew,
A school of porpoise flashed in view.
"Take, eat," he said, "and be content;
These fishes in my stead are sent
By Him who gave the tangled ram
To spare the child of Abraham."

Our uncle, innocent of books,
Was rich in lore of fields and brooks,
The ancient teachers never dumb
Of Nature's unhoused lyceum.
In moons and tides and weather wise,
He read the clouds as prophecies,
And foul or fair could well divine,
By many an occult hint and sign,
Holding the cunning-warded keys
To all the woodcraft mysteries;
Himself to Nature's heart so near
That all her voices in his ear
Of beast or bird had meanings clear,
Like Apollonius of old,
Who knew the tales the sparrows told,
Or Hermes, who interpreted
What the sage cranes of Nilus said;
A simple, guileless, childlike man,
Content to live where life began;

Strong only on his native grounds,
The little world of sights and sounds
Whose girdle was the parish bounds,
Whereof his fondly partial pride
The common features magnified,
As Surrey hills to mountains grew
In White of Selborne's loving view,—
He told how teal and loon he shot,
And how the eagle's eggs he got,
The feats on pond and river done,
The prodigies of rod and gun;
Till, warming with the tales he told,
Forgotten was the outside cold,
The bitter wind unheeded blew,
From ripening corn the pigeons flew,
The partridge drummed i' the wood, the mink
Went fishing down the river-brink.
In fields with bean or clover gay,
The woodchuck, like a hermit gray,
   Peered from the doorway of his cell;
The muskrat plied the mason's trade,
And tier by tier his mud-walls laid;
And from the shagbark overhead
   The grizzled squirrel dropped his shell.

Next, the dear aunt, whose smile of cheer
And voice in dreams I see and hear,—
The sweetest woman ever Fate
Perverse denied a household mate,
Who, lonely, homeless, not the less
Found peace in love's unselfishness,
And welcome wheresoe'er she went,

A calm and gracious element,
Whose presence seemed the sweet income
And womanly atmosphere of home,—
Called up her girlhood memories,
The huskings and the apple-bees,
The sleigh-rides and the summer sails,
Weaving through all the poor details
And homespun warp of circumstance
A golden woof-thread of romance.
For well she kept her genial mood
And simple faith of maidenhood;
Before her still a cloud-land lay,
The mirage loomed across her way;
The morning dew, that dries so soon
With others, glistened at her noon;
Through years of toil and soil and care,
From glossy tress to thin gray hair,
All unprofaned she held apart
The virgin fancies of the heart.
Be shame to him of woman born
Who hath for such but thought of scorn.

There, too, our elder sister plied
Her evening task the stand beside;
A full, rich nature, free to trust,
Truthful and almost sternly just,
Impulsive, earnest, prompt to act,
And make her generous thought a fact,
Keeping with many a light disguise
The secret of self-sacrifice.
O heart sore-tried! thou hast the best
That Heaven itself could give thee,—rest,

Rest from all bitter thoughts and things!
  How many a poor one's blessing went
  With thee beneath the low green tent
Whose curtain never outward swings!

As one who held herself a part
Of all she saw, and let her heart
  Against the household bosom lean,
Upon the motley-braided mat
Our youngest and our dearest sat,
Lifting her large, sweet, asking eyes,
  Now bathed in the unfading green
And holy peace of Paradise.
Oh, looking from some heavenly hill,
  Or from the shade of saintly palms,
  Or silver reach of river calms,
Do those large eyes behold me still?
With me one little year ago:—
The chill weight of the winter snow
  For months upon her grave has lain;
And now, when summer south-winds blow
  And brier and harebell bloom again,
I tread the pleasant paths we trod,
I see the violet-sprinkled sod
Whereon she leaned, too frail and weak
The hillside flowers she loved to seek,
Yet following me where'er I went
With dark eyes full of love's content.
The birds are glad; the brier-rose fills
The air with sweetness; all the hills
Stretch green to June's unclouded sky;
But still I wait with ear and eye,

For something gone which should be nigh,
A loss in all familiar things,
In flower that blooms, and bird that sings.
And yet, dear heart! remembering thee,
    Am I not richer than of old?
Safe in thy immortality,
    What change can reach the wealth I hold?
    What chance can mar the pearl and gold
Thy love hath left in trust with me?
And while in late life's afternoon,
    Where cool and long the shadows grow,
I walk to meet the night that soon
    Shall shape and shadow overflow,
I cannot feel that thou art far,
Since near at need the angels are;
And when the sunset gates unbar,
    Shall I not see thee waiting stand,
And, white against the evening star,
    The welcome of thy beckoning hand?

Brisk wielder of the birch and rule,
The master of the district school
Held at the fire his favored place,
Its warm glow lit a laughing face
Fresh-hued and fair, where scarce appeared
The uncertain prophecy of beard.
He teased the mitten-blinded cat,
Played cross-pins on my uncle's hat,
Sang songs, and told us what befalls
In classic Dartmouth's college halls.
Born the wild Northern hills among,
From whence his yeoman father wrung

By patient toil subsistence scant,
Not competence and yet not want,
He early gained the power to pay
His cheerful, self-reliant way;
Could doff at ease his scholar's gown
To peddle wares from town to town;
Or through the long vacation's reach
In lonely lowland districts teach,
Where all the droll experience found
At stranger hearths in boarding round,
The moonlit skater's keen delight,
The sleigh-drive through the frosty night,
The rustic party, with its rough
Accompaniment of blind-man's-buff,
And whirling-plate, and forfeits paid,
His winter task a pastime made.
Happy the snow-locked homes wherein
He tuned his merry violin,
Or played the athlete in the barn,
Or held the good dame's winding-yarn,
Or mirth-provoking versions told
Of classic legends rare and old,
Wherein the scenes of Greece and Rome
Had all the commonplace of home,
And little seemed at best the odds
'Twixt Yankee pedlers and old gods;
Where Pindus-born Arachthus took
The guise of any grist-mill brook,
And dread Olympus at his will
Became a huckleberry hill.

A careless boy that night he seemed;
  But at his desk he had the look
And air of one who wisely schemed,
  And hostage from the future took
  In trainëd thought and lore of book.
Large-brained, clear-eyed, of such as he
Shall Freedom's young apostles be,
Who, following in War's bloody trail,
Shall every lingering wrong assail;
All chains from limb and spirit strike,
Uplift the black and white alike;
Scatter before their swift advance
The darkness and the ignorance,
The pride, the lust, the squalid sloth,
Which nurtured Treason's monstrous growth,
Made murder pastime, and the hell
Of prison-torture possible;
The cruel lie of caste refute,
Old forms remould, and substitute
For Slavery's lash the freeman's will,
For blind routine, wise-handed skill;
A school-house plant on every hill,
Stretching in radiate nerve-lines thence
The quick wires of intelligence;
Till North and South together brought
Shall own the same electric thought,
In peace a common flag salute,
And, side by side in labor's free
And unresentful rivalry,
Harvest the fields wherein they fought.

*   *   *   *   *

At last the great logs, crumbling low,
Sent out a dull and duller glow,
The bull's-eye watch that hung in view,
Ticking its weary circuit through,
Pointed with mutely warning sign
Its black hand to the hour of nine.
That sign the pleasant circle broke:
My uncle ceased his pipe to smoke,
Knocked from its bowl the refuse gray,
And laid it tenderly away;
Then roused himself to safely cover
The dull red brands with ashes over.
And while, with care, our mother laid
The work aside, her steps she stayed
One moment, seeking to express
Her grateful sense of happiness
For food and shelter, warmth and health,
And love's contentment more than wealth,
With simple wishes (not the weak,
Vain prayers which no fulfilment seek,
But such as warm the generous heart,
O'er-prompt to do with Heaven its part)
That none might lack, that bitter night,
For bread and clothing, warmth and light.

Within our beds awhile we heard
The wind that round the gables roared,
With now and then a ruder shock,
Which made our very bedsteads rock.
We heard the loosened clapboards tost,
The board-nails snapping in the frost;
And on us, through the unplastered wall,
Felt the light sifted snow-flakes fall.

But sleep stole on, as sleep will do
When hearts are light and life is new;
Faint and more faint the murmurs grew,
Till in the summer-land of dreams
They softened to the sound of streams,
Low stir of leaves, and dip of oars,
And lapsing waves on quiet shores.

Next morn we wakened with the shout
Of merry voices high and clear;
And saw the teamsters drawing near
To break the drifted highways out.
Down the long hillside treading slow
We saw the half-buried oxen go,
Shaking the snow from heads uptost,
Their straining nostrils white with frost.
Before our door the straggling train
Drew up, an added team to gain.
The elders threshed their hands a-cold,
   Passed, with the cider-mug, their jokes
   From lip to lip; the younger folks
Down the loose snow-banks, wrestling rolled,
Then toiled again the cavalcade
   O'er windy hill, through clogged ravine,
   And woodland paths that wound between
Low drooping pine-boughs winter-weighed.
From every barn a team afoot,
At every house a new recruit,
Where, drawn by Nature's subtlest law,
Haply the watchful young men saw
Sweet doorway pictures of the curls
And curious eyes of merry girls,
Lifting their hands in mock defence

Against the snow-ball's compliments,
And reading in each missive tost
The charm with Eden never lost.

*   *   *   *   *

So days went on: a week had passed
Since the great world was heard from last.
The Almanac we studied o'er,
Read and reread our little store
Of books and pamphlets, scarce a score;
One harmless novel, mostly hid
From younger eyes, a book forbid,
And poetry, (or good or bad,
A single book was all we had,)
Where Ellwood's meek, drab-skirted Muse,
    A stranger to the heathen Nine,
    Sang, with a somewhat nasal whine,
The wars of David and the Jews.
At last the floundering carrier bore
The village paper to our door.
Lo! broadening outward as we read,
To warmer zones the horizon spread
In panoramic length unrolled
We saw the marvels that it told.
Before us passed the painted Creeks,
    And daft McGregor on his raids
    In Costa Rica's everglades.
And up Taygetos winding slow
Rode Ypsilanti's Mainote Greeks,
A Turk's head at each saddle-bow!
Welcome to us its week-old news,
Its corner for the rustic Muse,
    Its monthly gauge of snow and rain,

Its record, mingling in a breath
The wedding bell and dirge of death:
Jest, anecdote, and love-lorn tale,
The latest culprit sent to jail;
Its hue and cry of stolen and lost,
Its vendue sales and goods at cost,
  And traffic calling loud for gain.
We felt the stir of hall and street,
The pulse of life that round us beat;
The chill embargo of the snow
Was melted in the genial glow;
Wide swung again our ice-locked door,
And all the world was ours once more!

Clasp, Angel of the backward look
  And folded wings of ashen gray
  And voice of echoes far away,
The brazen covers of thy book;
The weird palimpsest old and vast,
Wherein thou hid'st the spectral past;
Where, closely mingling, pale and glow
The characters of joy and woe;
The monographs of outlived years,
Or smile-illumed or dim with tears,
  Green hills of life that slope to death,
And haunts of home, whose vistaed trees
Shade off to mournful cypresses
  With the white amaranths underneath.
Even while I look, I can but heed
  The restless sands' incessant fall,
Importunate hours that hours succeed,
Each clamorous with its own sharp need,
  And duty keeping pace with all.

Shut down and clasp with heavy lids;
I hear again the voice that bids
The dreamer leave his dream midway
For larger hopes and graver fears:
Life greatens in these later years,
The century's aloe flowers to-day!

Yet, haply, in some lull of life,
Some Truce of God which breaks its strife,
The wordling's eyes shall gather dew,
    Dreaming in throngful city ways
Of winter joys his boyhood knew;
And dear and early friends—the few
Who yet remain—shall pause to view
    These Flemish pictures of old days;
Sit with me by the homestead hearth
And stretch the hands of memory forth
    To warm them at the wood-fire's blaze!
And thanks untraced to lips unknown
Shall greet me like the odors blown
From unseen meadows newly mown,
Or lilies floating in some pond,
Wood-fringed, the wayside gaze beyond;
The traveller owns the grateful sense
Of sweetness near, he knows not whence,
And, pausing takes with forehead bare
The benediction of the air.

OLIVER WENDELL HOLMES
(1809-1894)

The reputation of the elder Holmes has languished in the shadow of his son, the eminent jurist, but his breadth and significance as an American poet is clear from the three examples below, each of which has made an important contribution to our cultural heritage.

"Old Ironsides," written when the poet was in his early twenties, was a popular call to save the famous U.S.S. *Constitution* (Holmes's own editorial note provides the context that gave rise to the poem). Its success as a rallying cry can be observed by anyone venturing to Boston Harbor, where the ship is still docked.

Old Ironsides
September 16, 1830

Ay, tear her tattered ensign down!
  Long has it waved on high,
And many an eye has danced to see
  That banner in the sky;
Beneath it rung the battle shout,
  And burst the cannon's roar;—
The meteor of the ocean air
  Shall sweep the clouds no more.

Her deck, once red with heroes' blood,
　Where knelt the vanquished foe,
When winds were hurrying o'er the flood,
　And waves were white below,
No more shall feel the victor's tread,
　Or know the conquered knee;—
The harpies of the shore shall pluck
　The eagle of the sea!

Oh, better that her shattered hulk
　Should sink beneath the wave;
Her thunders shook the mighty deep,
　And there should be her grave;
Nail to the mast her holy flag,
　Set every threadbare sail,
And give her to the god of storms,
　The lightning and the gale!

Author's Note
by Oliver Wendell Holmes

This was the popular name by which the frigate *Constitution* was known. The poem was first printed in the *Boston Daily Advertiser*, at the time when it was proposed to break up the old ship as unfit for service. I subjoin the paragraph which led to the writing of the poem. It is from the *Advertiser* of Tuesday, September 14, 1830:

> "Old Ironsides.—It has been affirmed upon good authority that the Secretary of the Navy has recommended to the Board of Navy Commissioners to dispose of the frigate *Constitution*. Since it has been understood that such a step was in contemplation we have heard but one opinion expressed, and that in decided disapprobation of the measure. Such a national object of interest, so endeared to our national pride as Old

Ironsides is, should never by any act of our government cease to belong to the Navy, so long as our country is to be found upon the map of nations. In England it was lately determined by the Admiralty to cut the *Victory*, a one-hundred gun ship (which it will be recollected bore the flag of Lord Nelson at the battle of Trafalgar), down to a seventy-four, but so loud were the lamentations of the people upon the proposed measure that the intention was abandoned. We confidently anticipate that the Secretary of the Navy will in like manner consult the general wish in regard to the *Constitution*, and either let her remain in ordinary or rebuild her whenever the public service may require."

—*New York Journal of Commerce*

Holmes was one of the so-called Boston Brahmins involved in the Transcendentalism movement, which, influenced both by Hindu traditions and European romanticism, found its inspiration in manifestations of nature. Here an abandoned crustacean's shell gives rise to an eloquent and moving reflection on the meaning of life. It's interesting to compare this poem to Longfellow's "A Psalm of Life," above.

The Chambered Nautilus

This is the ship of pearl, which, poets feign,
    Sails the unshadowed main,
    The venturous bark that flings
On the sweet summer wind its purpled wings
In gulfs enchanted, where the Siren sings,
    And coral reefs lie bare,
Where the cold sea-maids rise to sun their streaming hair.

Its webs of living gauze no more unfurl;
    Wrecked is the ship of pearl!
    And every chambered cell,
Where its dim dreaming life was wont to dwell,
As the frail tenant shaped his growing shell,
    Before thee lies revealed,
Its irised ceiling rent, its sunless crypt unsealed!

Year after year beheld the silent toil
    That spread his lustrous coil;
    Still, as the spiral grew,
He left the past year's dwelling for the new,
Stole with soft steps its shining archway through,
    Built up its idle door,
Stretched in his last-found home, and knew the old no more.

Thanks for the heavenly message brought by thee,
    Child of the wandering sea,
    Cast from her lap, forlorn!
From thy dead lips a clearer note is born
Than ever Triton blew from wreathéd horn!
    While on mine ear it rings,
Through the deep caves of thought I hear a voice that sings:

Build thee more stately mansions, O my soul,
    As the swift seasons roll!
    Leave thy low-vaulted past!
Let each new temple, nobler than the last,
Shut thee from heaven with a dome more vast,
    Till thou at length art free,
Leaving thine outgrown shell by life's unresting sea!

Perhaps the greatest example of American folk humor in poetic form, this verse is both a tribute to Yankee ingenuity and hard work and a masterpiece of logical nonsense.

The Deacon's Masterpiece, or The Wonderful "One-Hoss Shay"

Have you heard of the wonderful one-hoss shay,
That was built in such a logical way
It ran a hundred years to a day,
And then, of a sudden, it—ah, but stay,
I'll tell you what happened without delay,
Scaring the parson into fits,
Frightening people out of their wits,—
Have you ever heard of that, I say?

Seventeen hundred and fifty-five.
Georgius Secundus was then alive,—
Snuffy old drone from the German hive.
That was the year when Lisbon-town
Saw the earth open and gulp her down,
And Braddock's army was done so brown,
Left without a scalp to its crown.
It was on the terrible Earthquake-day
That the Deacon finished the one-hoss shay.

Now in building of chaises, I tell you what,
There is always *somewhere* a weaker spot,—

In hub, tire, felloe, in spring or thill,
In panel, or crossbar, or floor, or sill,
In screw, bolt, thoroughbrace,—lurking still,
Find it somewhere you must and will,—
Above or below, or within or without,—
And that's the reason, beyond a doubt,
A chaise *breaks down,* but doesn't *wear out.*

But the Deacon swore (as Deacons do,
With an "I dew vum," or an "I tell *yeou*")
He would build one shay to beat the taown
'N' the keounty 'n' all the kentry raoun';
It should be so built that it *couldn'* break daown:
"Fur," said the Deacon, "'t's mighty plain
Thut the weakes' place mus' stan' the strain;
'N' the way t' fix it, uz I maintain,
            Is only jest
T' make that place uz strong uz the rest."

So the Deacon inquired of the village folk
Where he could find the strongest oak,
That couldn't be split nor bent nor broke,—
That was for spokes and floor and sills;
He sent for lancewood to make the thills;
The crossbars were ash, from the straightest trees,
The panels of white-wood, that cuts like cheese,
But lasts like iron for things like these;
The hubs of logs from the "Settler's ellum,"—
Last of its timber,—they couldn't sell 'em,
Never an axe had seen their chips,
And the wedges flew from between their lips,
Their blunt ends frizzled like celery-tips;

Step and prop-iron, bolt and screw,
Spring, tire, axle, and linchpin too,
Steel of the finest, bright and blue;
Thoroughbrace bison-skin, thick and wide;
Boot, top, dasher, from tough old hide
Found in the pit when the tanner died.
That was the way he "put her through."—
"There!" said the Deacon, "naow she'll dew!"

Do! I tell you, I rather guess
She was a wonder, and nothing less!
Colts grew horses, beards turned gray,
Deacon and deaconess dropped away,
Children and grandchildren—where were they?
But there stood the stout old one-hoss shay
As fresh as on Lisbon-earthquake-day!

Eighteen hundred;—it came and found
The Deacon's masterpiece strong and sound.
Eighteen hundred increased by ten;—
"Hahnsum kerridge" they called it then.
Eighteen hundred and twenty came;—
Running as usual; much the same.
Thirty and forty at last arrive,
And then came fifty, and Fifty-five,

Little of all we value here
Wakes on the morn of its hundredth year
Without both feeling and looking queer.
In fact, there's nothing that keeps its youth,
So far as I know, but a tree and truth.
(This as a moral that runs at large;
Take it.—You're welcome.—No extra charge.)

First of November,—the Earthquake-day,—
There are traces of age in the one-hoss shay,
A general flavor of mild decay,
But nothing local, as one may say.
There couldn't be,—for the Deacon's art
Had made it so like in every part
That there wasn't a chance for one to start.
For the wheels were just as strong as the thills,
And the floor was just as strong as the sills,
And the panels just as strong as the floor,
And the whipple-tree neither less nor more,
And the back crossbar as strong as the fore,
And spring and axle and hub *encore,*
And yet, *as a whole,* it is past a doubt
In another hour it will be *worn out!*

First of November, 'Fifty-five!
This morning the parson takes a drive.
Now, small boys, get out of the way!
Here comes the wonderful one-hoss shay,
Drawn by a rat-tailed, ewe-necked bay.
"Huddup!" said the parson.—Off went they.
The parson was working his Sunday text,—
Had got to *fifthly,* and stopped perplexed
At what the—Moses—was coming next.
All at once the horse stood still,
Close by the meet'n'-house on the hill.
First a shiver, and then a thrill,
Then something decidedly like a spill,—
And the parson was sitting up on a rock,
At half past nine by the meet'n'-house clock,—
Just the hour of the Earthquake shock!
What do you think the parson found,

When he got up and stared around?
The poor old chaise in a heap or mound,
As if it had been to the mill and ground!
You see, of course, if you're not a dunce,
How it went to pieces all at once,—
All at once, and nothing first,—
Just as bubbles do when they burst.

End of the wonderful one-hoss shay.
Logic is logic. That's all I say.

EDGAR ALLAN POE

(1809–1849)

Poe died at forty, an impoverished alcoholic, but his gothic sensibility, so at odds with the American tradition he wrote in, was warmly embraced by Europeans (his works were translated into French by Baudelaire). During his lifetime he yearned in vain for the respectability and success of such establishment poets as Longfellow and James Russell Lowell, but today he is certainly more widely read than either, especially by young people. He taps an essential part of the adolescent soul—a dark-toned romanticism that equates love with loss, and finds the image of destruction not unappealing, especially when, as in "The Bells," it's evoked very loudly! (Of course, "To Helen" is a very sweet poem, but its classical allusions leave little doubt that the love it celebrates is quite idealized.)

The Raven

Once upon a midnight dreary, while I pondered, weak and weary,
Over many a quaint and curious volume of forgotten lore—
While I nodded, nearly napping, suddenly there came a tapping,
As of some one gently rapping, rapping at my chamber door.
"'Tis some visitor," I muttered, "tapping at my chamber door—
                              Only this, and nothing more."

Ah, distinctly I remember it was in the bleak December,
And each separate dying ember wrought its ghost upon the floor.
Eagerly I wished the morrow;—vainly I had sought to borrow
From my books surcease of sorrow—sorrow for the lost Lenore—
For the rare and radiant maiden whom the angels name Lenore
                              Nameless *here* for evermore.

And the silken, sad, uncertain rustling of each purple curtain
Thrilled me—filled me with fantastic terrors never felt before;
So that now, to still the beating of my heart, I stood repeating,
" 'Tis some visitor entreating entrance at my chamber door—
Some late visitor entreating entrance at my chamber door;—
                              This it is, and nothing more."

Presently my soul grew stronger; hesitating then no longer,
"Sir," said I, "or Madam, truly your forgiveness I implore;
But the fact is I was napping, and so gently you came rapping,
And so faintly you came tapping, tapping at my chamber door,
That I scarce was sure I heard you"—here I opened wide the door;
                              Darkness there and nothing more.

Deep into that darkness peering, long I stood there wondering, fearing,
Doubting, dreaming dreams no mortal ever dared to dream before;
But the silence was unbroken, and the stillness gave no token,
And the only word there spoken was the whispered word, "Lenore?"
This I whispered, and an echo murmured back the word, "Lenore!"—
                              Merely this, and nothing more.

Back into the chamber turning, all my soul within me burning,
Soon again I heard a tapping somewhat louder than before.
"Surely," said I, "surely that is something at my window lattice;
Let me see, then, what thereat is, and this mystery explore—
Let my heart be still a moment and this mystery explore;—
'Tis the wind and nothing more!"

Open here I flung the shutter, when, with many a flirt and flutter,
In there stepped a stately Raven of the saintly days of yore;
Not the least obeisance made he; not a minute stopped or stayed he;
But, with mien of lord or lady, perched above my chamber door—
Perched upon a bust of Pallas just above my chamber door
Perched, and sat, and nothing more.

Then this ebony bird beguiling my sad fancy into smiling,
By the grave and stern decorum of the countenance it wore,
"Though thy crest be shorn and shaven, thou," I said, "art sure no
craven,
Ghastly grim and ancient Raven wandering from the Nightly shore—
Tell me what thy lordly name is on the Night's Plutonian shore!"
Quoth the Raven, "Nevermore."

Much I marvelled this ungainly fowl to hear discourse so plainly,
Though its answer little meaning—little relevancy bore;
For we cannot help agreeing that no living human being
Ever yet was blest with seeing bird above his chamber door—
Bird or beast upon the sculptured bust above his chamber door,
With such name as "Nevermore."

But the Raven, sitting lonely on the placid bust, spoke only
That one word, as if his soul in that one word he did outpour.
Nothing farther then he uttered—not a feather then he fluttered—
Till I scarcely more than muttered, "Other friends have flown before—
On the morrow *he* will leave me, as my Hopes have flown before."
Then the bird said, "Nevermore."

Startled at the stillness broken by reply so aptly spoken,
"Doubtless," said I, "what it utters is its only stock and store
Caught from some unhappy master whom unmerciful Disaster
Followed fast and followed faster till his songs one burden bore—
Till the dirges of his Hope that melancholy burden bore
Of 'Never—nevermore.'"

But the Raven still beguiling my sad fancy into smiling,
Straight I wheeled a cushioned seat in front of bird, and bust and door;
Then, upon the velvet sinking, I betook myself to linking
Fancy unto fancy, thinking what this ominous bird of yore—
What this grim, ungainly, ghastly, gaunt, and ominous bird of yore
Meant in croaking "Nevermore."

This I sat engaged in guessing, but no syllable expressing
To the fowl whose fiery eyes now burned into my bosom's core;
This and more I sat divining, with my head at ease reclining
On the cushion's velvet lining that the lamp-light gloated o'er,
But whose velvet-violet lining with the lamp-light gloating o'er,
She shall press, ah, nevermore!

Then, methought the air grew denser, perfumed from an unseen censer
Swung by seraphim whose foot-falls tinkled on the tufted floor.
"Wretch," I cried, "thy God hath lent thee—by these angels he hath sent thee
Respite—respite and nepenthe, from thy memories of Lenore;
Quaff, oh quaff this kind nepenthe and forget this lost Lenore!"
                    Quoth the Raven, "Nevermore."

"Prophet!" said I, "thing of evil!—prophet still, if bird or devil!—
Whether Tempter sent, or whether tempest tossed thee here ashore,
Desolate yet all undaunted, on this desert land enchanted—
On this home by Horror haunted—tell me truly, I implore—
Is there—*is* there balm in Gilead?—tell me—tell me, I implore!"
                    Quoth the Raven, "Nevermore."

"Prophet!" said I, "thing of evil—prophet still, if bird or devil!
By that Heaven that bends above us—by that God we both adore—
Tell this soul with sorrow laden if, within the distant Aidenn,
It shall clasp a sainted maiden whom the angels name Lenore—
Clasp a rare and radiant maiden whom the angels name Lenore."
                    Quoth the Raven, "Nevermore."

"Be that word our sign in parting, bird or fiend," I shrieked, upstarting—
"Get thee back into the tempest and the Night's Plutonian shore!
Leave no black plume as a token of that lie thy soul hath spoken!
Leave my loneliness unbroken!—quit the bust above my door!
Take thy beak from out my heart, and take thy form from off my door!"
                    Quoth the Raven, "Nevermore."

And the Raven, never flitting, still is sitting, *still* is sitting
On the pallid bust of Pallas just above my chamber door;
And his eyes have all the seeming of a demon's that is dreaming,
And the lamp-light o'er him streaming throws his shadow on the floor;
And my soul from out that shadow that lies floating on the floor

Shall be lifted—nevermore!

Poe wrote two poems with this title, but this is by far the more accomplished and famous. It was dedicated to the mother of a childhood friend, but clearly it evokes the most famous beauty of classical legend, Helen of Troy.

To Helen

Helen, thy beauty is to me
  Like those Nicéan barks of yore,
That gently, o'er a perfumed sea,
  The weary, way-worn wanderer bore
  To his own native shore.

On desperate seas long wont to roam,
  Thy hyacinth hair, thy classic face,
Thy Naiad airs have brought me home
  To the glory that was Greece,
  And the grandeur that was Rome.

Lo! in that little window-niche
  How statue-like I see thee stand,
The agate lamp within thy hand!
Ah! Psyche, from the regions which
Are Holy land!

Perhaps the greatest example of onomatopoeia in our literature.

The Bells

I

HEAR the sledges with the bells—
Silver bells!
What a world of merriment their melody foretells!
How they tinkle, tinkle, tinkle,
In the icy air of night!
While the stars that oversprinkle
All the heavens, seem to twinkle
With a crystalline delight;
Keeping time, time, time,
In a sort of Runic rhyme,
To the tintinnabulation that so musically wells
From the bells, bells, bells, bells,
Bells, bells, bells—
From the jingling and the tinkling of the bells.

II

Hear the mellow wedding bells—
Golden bells!
What a world of happiness their harmony foretells!
Through the balmy air of night
How they ring out their delight!—
From the molten-golden notes,

And all in tune,
What a liquid ditty floats
To the turtle-dove that listens, while she gloats
On the moon!
Oh, from out the sounding cells,
What a gush of euphony voluminously wells!
How it swells!
How it dwells
On the Future! how it tells
Of the rapture that impels
To the swinging and the ringing
Of the bells, bells, bells,
Of the bells, bells, bells, bells,
Bells, bells, bells—
To the rhyming and the chiming of the bells!

III

Hear the loud alarum bells—
Brazen bells!
What tale of terror, now, their turbulency tells!
In the startled ear of night
How they scream out their affright!
Too much horrified to speak,
They can only shriek, shriek,
Out of tune,
In a clamorous appealing to the mercy of the fire,
In a mad expostulation with the deaf and frantic fire,
Leaping higher, higher, higher,
With a desperate desire,
And a resolute endeavor
Now—now to sit or never,
By the side of the pale-faced moon.

Oh, the bells, bells, bells!
What a tale their terror tells
Of despair!
How they clang, and clash, and roar!
What a horror they outpour
On the bosom of the palpitating air!
Yet the ear, it fully knows,
By the twanging,
And the clanging,
How the danger ebbs and flows;
Yet, the ear distinctly tells,
In the jangling,
And the wrangling,
How the danger sinks and swells,
By the sinking or the swelling in the anger of the bells—
Of the bells—
Of the bells, bells, bells, bells,
Bells, bells, bells—
In the clamor and the clangor of the bells!

IV

Hear the tolling of the bells—
Iron bells!
What a world of solemn thought their monody compels!
In the silence of the night,
How we shiver with affright
At the melancholy meaning of their tone!
For every sound that floats
From the rust within their throats
Is a groan.
And the people—ah, the people—
They that dwell up in the steeple,

All alone,
And who, tolling, tolling, tolling,
In that muffled monotone,
Feel a glory in so rolling
On the human heart a stone—
They are neither man nor woman—
They are neither brute nor human—
They are Ghouls:
And their king it is who tolls;—
And he rolls, rolls, rolls, rolls,
Rolls
A pæan from the bells!
And his merry bosom swells
With the pæan of the bells!
And he dances, and he yells;
Keeping time, time, time,
In a sort of Runic rhyme,
To the pæan of the bells—
Of the bells:
Keeping time, time, time,
In a sort of Runic rhyme,
To the throbbing of the bells—
Of the bells, bells, bells—
To the sobbing of the bells;
Keeping time, time, time,
As he knells, knells, knells,
In a happy Runic rhyme,
To the rolling of the bells—
Of the bells, bells, bells—
To the tolling of the bells—
Of the bells, bells, bells, bells—
Bells, bells, bells—
To the moaning and the groaning of the bells.

JAMES RUSSELL LOWELL

(1819–1891)

James Russell Lowell was a member of America's cultural ruling class. At a time when Boston was considered the Hub of the Nation (a nickname that has continued to this day), a popular verse denoted its elite:

> *Hurrah for the City of Boston,*
> *The Land of the Bean and the Cod,*
> *Where the Cabots speak only to Lowells,*
> *And the Lowells speak only to God.*

Lowell was known in his time not only as a poet, but as a journalist (he was one of the founders of the *Atlantic Monthly*), literary critic, and abolitionist. Today he is little read, but he, Longfellow, and Whittier were among the writers making up the American literary canon of their time. Despite his subsequent fall into obscurity, it's undeniable that the poem below, remembered today mainly for its first two lines, helped contribute to what is now a traditional sense of an idyllic America always on the brink of summer.

What Is So Rare As a Day in June
from "The Vision of Sir Launfal"

And what is so rare as a day in June?
   Then, if ever, come perfect days;
Then Heaven tries earth if it be in tune,
   And over it softly her warm ear lays;
Whether we look, or whether we listen,

We hear life murmur, or see it glisten;
Every clod feels a stir of might,
   An instinct within it that reaches and towers,
And, groping blindly above it for light,
   Climbs to a soul in grass and flowers;
The flush of life may well be seen
   Thrilling back over hills and valleys;
The cowslip startles in meadows green,
   The buttercup catches the sun in its chalice,
And there's never a leaf nor a blade too mean
   To be some happy creature's palace;
The little bird sits at his door in the sun,
   Atilt like a blossom among the leaves,
And lets his illumined being o'errun
   With the deluge of summer it receives;
His mate feels the eggs beneath her wings,
And the heart in her dumb breast flutters and sings;
He sings to the wide world, and she to her nest,—
In the nice ear of Nature which song is the best?

Now is the high-tide of the year,
   And whatever of life hath ebbed away
Comes flooding back with a ripply cheer,
   Into every bare inlet and creek and bay;
Now the heart is so full that a drop overfills it,
We are happy now because God wills it;
No matter how barren the past may have been,
'Tis enough for us now that the leaves are green;
We sit in the warm shade and feel right well
How the sap creeps up and the blossoms swell;
We may shut our eyes but we cannot help knowing
That skies are clear and grass is growing;
The breeze comes whispering in our ear,

That dandelions are blossoming near,
   That maize has sprouted, that streams are flowing,
That the river is bluer than the sky,
That the robin is plastering his house hard by;
And if the breeze kept the good news back,
For our couriers we should not lack;
   We could guess it all by yon heifer's lowing,—
And hark! how clear bold chanticleer,
Warmed with the new wine of the year,
   Tells all in his lusty crowing!

Joy comes, grief goes, we know not how;
Everything is happy now,
   Everything is upward striving;
'Tis as easy now for the heart to be true
As for grass to be green or skies to be blue,—
   'Tis for the natural way of living:
Who knows whither the clouds have fled?
   In the unscarred heaven they leave no wake,
And the eyes forget the tears they have shed,
   The heart forgets its sorrow and ache;
The soul partakes the season's youth,
   And the sulphurous rifts of passion and woe
Lie deep 'neath a silence pure and smooth,
   Like burnt-out craters healed with snow.

HERMAN MELVILLE

(1819–1891)

In this poem by Melville, the tone, diction, and subject matter of American poetry has clearly changed. Though the poem was written some years before the poet's death, and is thought to have preceded the novel *Billy Budd*, of which it now forms the conclusion, neither the novel nor the poem was published until 1924, more than three decades after Melville died. The poem is rhymed, but the rhyme is not intrusive, as the narrator dreamingly contemplates his imminent death at sea. At the end it's possible to detect a hint of Ariel's song in *The Tempest*, "Full Fathom Five Thy Father Lies." Certainly this poem, like Shakespeare's, is about transformation, and in reading it one can almost sense, as in much of Melville's fiction, the ongoing transformation of the certitudes of the traditional nineteenth-century world into a more complex, and certainly darker, future.

Billy in the Darbies

Good of the Chaplain to enter Lone Bay
And down on his marrowbones here and pray
For the likes just o' me, Billy Budd.—But look:
Through the port comes the moonshine astray!
It tips the guard's cutlass and silvers this nook;
But 'twill die in the dawning of Billy's last day.
A jewel-block they'll make of me tomorrow,
Pendant pearl from the yardarm-end
Like the eardrop I gave to Bristol Molly—

O, 'tis me, not the sentence they'll suspend.

Ay, ay, all is up; and I must up too,

Early in the morning, aloft from alow.

On an empty stomach now never it would do.

They'll give me a nibble—bit o' biscuit ere I go.

Sure, a messmate will reach me the last parting cup;

But, turning heads away from the hoist and the belay,

Heaven knows who will have the running of me up!

No pipe to those halyards.—But aren't it all sham?

A blur's in my eyes; it is dreaming that I am.

A hatchet to my hawser? All adrift to go?

The drum roll to grog, and Billy never know?

But Donald he has promised to stand by the plank;

So I'll shake a friendly hand ere I sink.

But—no! It is dead then I'll be, come to think.

I remember Taff the Welshman when he sank.

And his cheek it was like the budding pink.

But me they'll lash in hammock, drop me deep.

Fathoms down, fathoms down, how I'll dream fast asleep.

I feel it stealing now. Sentry, are you there?

Just ease these darbies at the wrist,

And roll me over fair!

I am sleepy, and the oozy weeds about me twist.

WALT WHITMAN
(1819–1892)

When Whitman sent an advance copy of the first edition of *Leaves of Grass* to Ralph Waldo Emerson in 1855, Emerson, one of the most prominent literary figures in the nation, responded with a letter praising the poems for their extraordinary originality, power, and wisdom. Clearly aware of the impact of this sort of acceptance by Emerson, Whitman, without permission, excerpted a line from the letter ("I greet you at the beginning of a great career") and printed it on the cover of the next edition of his revolutionary book of poems, possibly the most significant case of blurbing in American publishing history!

Whitman is the greatest American poet for any number of reasons. First there is his voice, unmistakable and powerful, almost biblical in its authority. His poetry is largely unconcerned with rhyme, and its meter embodies the rhythm of the declamatory human voice, with an apparent naturalness that was far from artless. And what does that voice declaim? Whitman begins by celebrating himself, but soon moves on to the rest of the universe, with particular attention to the diversity and individuality of the American people around him. He writes about life and death, but also of the present and how it will become both the past and the future, changing but remaining the same. He writes in an earthy, personal way, and also in a transcendent address to eternity. He writes of sensuality and of the spirit, of Abraham Lincoln and of a child in the grass. John Dryden famously said of the work of Geoffrey Chaucer that "here is God's plenty." The words could equally apply to the great works of Walt Whitman, which, among their accomplishments, forever changed our ideas about the nature and limitations of poetry.

What is the grass
from *Leaves of Grass*

A child said, What is the grass? fetching it to me with full hands;
How could I answer the child? . . . . I do not know what it is any
    more than he.

I guess it must be the flag of my disposition,
     out of hopeful green stuff woven.

Or I guess it is the handkerchief of the Lord,
A scented gift and remembrancer designedly dropped,
Bearing the owner's name someway in the corners,
     that we may see and remark, and say Whose?

Or I guess the grass is itself a child . . . . the produced babe of the
    vegetation.

Or I guess it is a uniform hieroglyphic,
And it means, Sprouting alike in broad zones and narrow zones,
Growing among black folks as among white,
Kanuck, Tuckahoe, Congressman, Cuff, I give them the same,
     I receive them the same.

And now it seems to me the beautiful uncut hair of graves.

Tenderly will I use you curling grass,
It may be you transpire from the breasts of young men,
It may be if I had known them I would have loved them;
It may be you are from old people and from women, and from
     offspring taken soon out of their mothers' laps,
And here you are the mothers' laps.

This grass is very dark to be from the white heads of old mothers,
Darker than the colorless beards of old men,
Dark to come from under the faint red roofs of mouths.

O I perceive after all so many uttering tongues!
And I perceive they do not come from the roofs of mouths for
  nothing.

I wish I could translate the hints about the dead young men and
  women,
And the hints about old men and mothers, and the offspring taken
  soon out of their laps.

What do you think has become of the young and old men?
What do you think has become of the women and children?

They are alive and well somewhere;
The smallest sprout shows there is really no death,
And if ever there was it led forward life, and does not wait at the end
  to arrest it,
And ceased the moment life appeared.

All goes onward and outward . . . . and nothing collapses,
And to die is different from what any one supposed, and luckier.

In this work, Whitman expresses his sense of the eternal, which includes continuity of spirit. This is a recurring theme in his poetry, as can be seen from the last lines of the preceding poem.

Out of the Cradle Endlessly Rocking

Out of the cradle endlessly rocking,
Out of the mocking-bird's throat, the musical shuttle,
Out of the Ninth-month midnight,
Over the sterile sands and the fields beyond, where the child leaving
    his bed wander'd alone, bareheaded, barefoot,
Down from the shower'd halo,
Up from the mystic play of shadows twining and twisting as if they
    were alive,
Out from the patches of briers and blackberries,
From the memories of the bird that chanted to me,
From your memories sad brother, from the fitful risings and fallings
    I heard,
From under that yellow half-moon late-risen and swollen as if with
    tears,
From those beginning notes of yearning and love there in the mist,
From the thousand responses of my heart never to cease,
From the myriad thence-arous'd words,
From the word stronger and more delicious than any,
From such as now they start the scene revisiting,
As a flock, twittering, rising, or overhead passing,
Borne hither, ere all eludes me, hurriedly,
A man, yet by these tears a little boy again,
Throwing myself on the sand, confronting the waves,

I, chanter of pains and joys, uniter of here and hereafter,
Taking all hints to use them, but swiftly leaping beyond them,
A reminiscence sing.

Once, Paumanok,
When the lilac-scent was in the air and Fifth-month grass was
    growing,
Up this seashore in some briers,
Two feather'd guests from Alabama, two together,
And their nest, and four light-green eggs spotted with brown,
And every day the he-bird to and fro near at hand,
And every day the she-bird crouch'd on her nest, silent, with bright
    eyes,
And every day I, a curious boy, never too close, never disturbing
    them,
Cautiously peering, absorbing, translating.

Shine! shine! shine!
Pour down your warmth, great sun!
While we bask, we two together.

Two together!
Winds blow south, or winds blow north,
Day come white, or night come black,
Home, or rivers and mountains from home,
Singing all time, minding no time,
While we two keep together.

Till of a sudden,
May-be kill'd, unknown to her mate,
One forenoon the she-bird crouch'd not on the nest,
Nor return'd that afternoon, nor the next,
Nor ever appear'd again.

And thenceforward all summer in the sound of the sea,
And at night under the full of the moon in calmer weather,
Over the hoarse surging of the sea,
Or flitting from brier to brier by day,
I saw, I heard at intervals the remaining one, the he-bird,
The solitary guest from Alabama.

Blow! blow! blow!
Blow up sea-winds along Paumanok's shore;
I wait and I wait till you blow my mate to me.

Yes, when the stars glisten'd,
All night long on the prong of a moss-scallop'd stake,
Down almost amid the slapping waves,
Sat the lone singer, wonderful, causing tears.

He call'd on his mate,
He pour'd forth the meanings which I of all men know.

Yes my brother I know,
The rest might not, but I have treasur'd every note,
For more than once dimly down to the beach gliding,
Silent, avoiding the moonbeams, blending myself with the shadows,
Recalling now the obscure shapes, the echoes, the sounds and sights
    after their sorts,
The white arms out in the breakers tirelessly tossing,
I, with bare feet, a child, the wind wafting my hair,
Listen'd long and long.

Listen'd to keep, to sing, now translating the notes,
Following you my brother.

Soothe! soothe! soothe!
Close on its wave soothes the wave behind,
And again another behind embracing and lapping, every one close,
But my love soothes not me, not me.

Low hangs the moon, it rose late,
It is lagging—O I think it is heavy with love, with love.

O madly the sea pushes upon the land,
With love, with love.

O night! do I not see my love fluttering out among the breakers?
What is that little black thing I see there in the white?

Loud! loud! loud!
Loud I call to you, my love!
High and clear I shoot my voice over the waves,
Surely you must know who is here, is here,
You must know who I am, my love.

Low-hanging moon!
What is that dusky spot in your brown yellow?
O it is the shape, the shape of my mate!
O moon do not keep her from me any longer.

Land! land! O land!
Whichever way I turn, O I think you could give me my mate back
   again if you only would,
For I am almost sure I see her dimly whichever way I look.

O rising stars!
Perhaps the one I want so much will rise, will rise with some of you.

O throat! O trembling throat!
Sound clearer through the atmosphere!
Pierce the woods, the earth,
Somewhere listening to catch you must be the one I want.

Shake out carols!
Solitary here, the night's carols!
Carols of lonesome love! death's carols!
Carols under that lagging, yellow, waning moon!
O under that moon where she droops almost down into the sea!
O reckless despairing carols.

But soft! sink low!
Soft! let me just murmur,
And do you wait a moment you husky-nois'd sea,
For somewhere I believe I heard my mate responding to me,
So faint, I must be still, be still to listen,
But not altogether still, for then she might not come immediately
    to me.

Hither my love!
Here I am! here!
With this just-sustain'd note I announce myself to you,
This gentle call is for you my love, for you.

Do not be decoy'd elsewhere,
That is the whistle of the wind, it is not my voice,
That is the fluttering, the fluttering of the spray,
Those are the shadows of leaves.

O darkness! O in vain!
O I am very sick and sorrowful.

O brown halo in the sky near the moon, drooping upon the sea!
O troubled reflection in the sea!
O throat! O throbbing heart!
And I singing uselessly, uselessly all the night.

O past! O happy life! O songs of joy!
In the air, in the woods, over fields,
Loved! loved! loved! loved! loved!
But my mate no more, no more with me!
We two together no more.

The aria sinking,
All else continuing, the stars shining,
The winds blowing, the notes of the bird continuous echoing,
With angry moans the fierce old mother incessantly moaning,
On the sands of Paumanok's shore gray and rustling,
The yellow half-moon enlarged, sagging down, drooping, the face of
    the sea almost touching,
The boy ecstatic, with his bare feet the waves, with his hair the
    atmosphere dallying,
The love in the heart long pent, now loose, now at last tumultuously
    bursting,
The aria's meaning, the ears, the soul, swiftly depositing,
The strange tears down the cheeks coursing,
The colloquy there, the trio, each uttering,
The undertone, the savage old mother incessantly crying,
To the boy's soul's questions sullenly timing, some drown'd secret
    hissing,
To the outsetting bard.

Demon or bird! (said the boy's soul,)
Is it indeed toward your mate you sing? or is it really to me?
For I, that was a child, my tongue's use sleeping, now I have heard
    you,
Now in a moment I know what I am for, I awake,
And already a thousand singers, a thousand songs, clearer, louder
    and more sorrowful than yours,
A thousand warbling echoes have started to life within me, never
    to die.

O you singer solitary, singing by yourself, projecting me,
O solitary me listening, never more shall I cease perpetuating you,
Never more shall I escape, never more the reverberations,
Never more the cries of unsatisfied love be absent from me,
Never again leave me to be the peaceful child I was before what
    there in the night,
By the sea under the yellow and sagging moon,
The messenger there arous'd, the fire, the sweet hell within,
The unknown want, the destiny of me.

O give me the clew! (it lurks in the night here somewhere,)
O if I am to have so much, let me have more!

A word then, (for I will conquer it,)
The word final, superior to all,
Subtle, sent up—what is it?—I listen;
Are you whispering it, and have been all the time, you sea-waves?
Is that it from your liquid rims and wet sands?

Whereto answering, the sea,

Delaying not, hurrying not,

Whisper'd me through the night, and very plainly before daybreak,

Lisp'd to me the low and delicious word death,

And again death, death, death, death,

Hissing melodious, neither like the bird nor like my arous'd child's
    heart,

But edging near as privately for me rustling at my feet,

Creeping thence steadily up to my ears and laving me softly all over,

Death, death, death, death, death.

Which I do not forget.

But fuse the song of my dusky demon and brother,

That he sang to me in the moonlight on Paumanok's gray beach,

With the thousand responsive songs at random,

My own songs awaked from that hour,

And with them the key, the word up from the waves,

The word of the sweetest song and all songs,

That strong and delicious word which, creeping to my feet,

(Or like some old crone rocking the cradle, swathed in sweet
    garments, bending aside,)

The sea whisper'd me.

In this poem Whitman, witnessing the present, projects himself into a far future in which he still discerns the continuity of life and spirit. The ferry was discontinued in 1924, more than twenty years after the opening of the Brooklyn Bridge.

Crossing Brooklyn Ferry

1

Flood-tide below me! I see you face to face!
Clouds of the west—sun there half an hour high—I see you also
    face to face.

Crowds of men and women attired in the usual costumes, how
    curious you are to me!
On the ferry-boats the hundreds and hundreds that cross, returning
    home, are more curious to me than you suppose,
And you that shall cross from shore to shore years hence are more to
    me, and more in my meditations, than you might suppose.

2

The impalpable sustenance of me from all things at all hours of the
    day,
The simple, compact, well-join'd scheme, myself disintegrated, every
    one disintegrated yet part of the scheme,
The similitudes of the past and those of the future,
The glories strung like beads on my smallest sights and hearings, on
    the walk in the street and the passage over the river,

The current rushing so swiftly and swimming with me far away,
The others that are to follow me, the ties between me and them,
The certainty of others, the life, love, sight, hearing of others.

Others will enter the gates of the ferry and cross from shore to
    shore,
Others will watch the run of the flood-tide,
Others will see the shipping of Manhattan north and west, and the
    heights of Brooklyn to the south and east,
Others will see the islands large and small;
Fifty years hence, others will see them as they cross, the sun half an
    hour high,
A hundred years hence, or ever so many hundred years hence, others
    will see them,
Will enjoy the sunset, the pouring-in of the flood-tide, the falling-
    back to the sea of the ebb-tide.

3

It avails not, time nor place—distance avails not,
I am with you, you men and women of a generation, or ever so many
    generations hence,
Just as you feel when you look on the river and sky, so I felt,
Just as any of you is one of a living crowd, I was one of a crowd,
Just as you are refreshed by the gladness of the river and the bright
    flow, I was refreshed,
Just as you stand and lean on the rail, yet hurry with the swift
    current, I stood yet was hurried,
Just as you look on the numberless masts of ships and the thick-
    stemm'd pipes of steamboats, I look'd.

I too many and many a time cross'd the river of old,
Watched the Twelfth-month seagulls, saw them high in the air
    floating with motionless wings, oscillating their bodies,
Saw how the glistening yellow lit up parts of their bodies and left the
    rest in strong shadow,
Saw the slow-wheeling circles and the gradual edging toward the
    south,
Saw the reflection of the summer sky in the water,
Had my eyes dazzled by the shimmering track of beams,
Look'd at the fine centrifugal spokes of light round the shape of my
    head in the sunlit water,
Look'd on the haze on the hills southward and south-westward,
Look'd on the vapor as it flew in fleeces tinged with violet,
Look'd toward the lower bay to notice the vessels arriving,
Saw their approach, saw aboard those that were near me,
Saw the white sails of schooners and sloops, saw the ships at
    anchor,
The sailors at work in the rigging or out astride the spars,
The round masts, the swinging motion of the hulls, the slender
    serpentine pennants,
The large and small steamers in motion, the pilots in their pilot-
    houses,
The white wake left by the passage, the quick tremulous whirl of the
    wheels,
The flags of all nations, the falling of them at sunset,
The scallop-edged waves in the twilight, the ladled cups, the
    frolicsome crests and glistening,
The stretch afar growing dimmer and dimmer, the gray walls of the
    granite storehouses by the docks,
On the river the shadowy group, the big steam-tug closely flank'd on
    each side by the barges, the hay-boat, the belated lighter,
On the neighboring shore the fires from the foundry chimneys
    burning high and glaringly into the night,

Casting their flicker of black contrasted with wild red and yellow
    light over the tops of houses, and down into the clefts of
    streets.

4

These and all else were to me the same as they are to you,
I loved well those cities, loved well the stately and rapid river,
The men and women I saw were all near to me,
Others the same—others who look back on me because I looked
    forward to them,
(The time will come, though I stop here to-day, and to-night.)

5

What is it then between us?
What is the count of the scores or hundreds of years between us?

Whatever it is, it avails not—distance avails not, and place avails
    not,
I too lived, Brooklyn of ample hills was mine,
I too walk'd the streets of Manhattan island, and bathed in the
    waters around it,
I too felt the curious abrupt questionings stir within me,
In the day among crowds of people sometimes they came
    upon me,
In my walks home late at night or as I lay in my bed they came
    upon me,
I too had been struck from the float forever held in solution,
I too had receiv'd identity by my body,
That I was, I knew was of my body—and what I should be, I knew I
    should be of my body.

6

It is not upon you alone the dark patches fall,
The dark threw its patches down upon me also,
The best I had done seemed to me blank and suspicious,
My great thoughts as I supposed them, were they not in reality
    meagre?
Nor is it you alone who know what it is to be evil,
I am he who knew what it was to be evil,
I too knitted the old knot of contrariety,
Blabb'd, blush'd, resented, lied, stole, grudg'd,
Had guile, anger, lust, hot wishes I dared not speak,
Was wayward, vain, greedy, shallow, sly, cowardly, malignant,
The wolf, the snake, the hog, not wanting in me,
The cheating look, the frivolous word, the adulterous wish, not
    wanting,
Refusals, hates, postponements, meanness, laziness, none of these
    wanting,
Was one with the rest, the days and haps of the rest,
Was call'd by my nighest name by clear loud voices of young men as
    they saw me approaching or passing,
Felt their arms on my neck as I stood, or the negligent leaning of
    their flesh against me as I sat,
Saw many I loved in the street or ferry-boat or public assembly, yet
    never told them a word,
Lived the same life with the rest, the same old laughing, gnawing,
    sleeping,
Played the part that still looks back on the actor or actress,
The same old role, the role that is what we make it, as great as we
    like,
Or as small as we like, or both great and small.

7

Closer yet I approach you,
What thought you have of me now, I had as much of you—I laid in
    my stores in advance,
I considered long and seriously of you before you were born.

Who was to know what should come home to me?
Who knows but I am enjoying this?
Who knows, for all the distance, but I am as good as looking at you
    now, for all you cannot see me?

8

Ah, what can ever be more stately and admirable to me than mast-
    hemm'd Manhattan?
River and sunset and scallop-edg'd waves of flood-tide?
The sea-gulls oscillating their bodies, the hay-boat in the twilight,
    and the belated lighter?
What gods can exceed these that clasp me by the hand, and with
    voices I love call me promptly and loudly by my nighest name as I
    approach?
What is more subtle than this which ties me to the woman or man
    that looks in my face?
Which fuses me into you now, and pours my meaning into you?

We understand then do we not?
What I promis'd without mentioning it, have you not accepted?
What the study could not teach—what the preaching could not
    accomplish is accomplished, is it not?

9

Flow on, river! flow with the flood-tide, and ebb with the ebb-tide!

Frolic on, crested and scallop-edg'd waves!

Gorgeous clouds of the sunset! drench with your splendor me, or the men and women generations after me!

Cross from shore to shore, countless crowds of passengers!

Stand up, tall masts of Mannahatta! stand up, beautiful hills of Brooklyn!

Throb, baffled and curious brain! throw out questions and answers!

Suspend here and everywhere, eternal float of solution!

Gaze, loving and thirsting eyes, in the house or street or public assembly!

Sound out, voices of young men! loudly and musically call me by my nighest name!

Live, old life! play the part that looks back on the actor or actress!

Play the old role, the role that is great or small according as one makes it!

Consider, you who peruse me, whether I may not in unknown ways be looking upon you;

Be firm, rail over the river, to support those who lean idly, yet haste with the hasting current;

Fly on, sea-birds! fly sideways, or wheel in large circles high in the air;

Receive the summer sky, you water, and faithfully hold it till all downcast eyes have time to take it from you!

Diverge, fine spokes of light, from the shape of my head, or any one's head, in the sunlit water!

Come on, ships from the lower bay! pass up or down, white-sail'd schooners, sloops, lighters!

Flaunt away, flags of all nations! be duly lower'd at sunset!

Burn high your fires, foundry chimneys! cast black shadows at nightfall! cast red and yellow light over the tops of the houses!

Appearances, now or henceforth, indicate what you are,

You necessary film, continue to envelop the soul,

About my body for me, and your body for you, be hung our divinest aromas,

Thrive, cities—bring your freight, bring your shows, ample and sufficient rivers,

Expand, being than which none else is perhaps more spiritual,

Keep your places, objects than which none else is more lasting.

You have waited, you always wait, you dumb, beautiful ministers,

We receive you with free sense at last, and are insatiate henceforward,

Not you any more shall be able to foil us, or withhold yourselves from us,

We use you, and do not cast you aside—we plant you permanently within us,

We fathom you not—we love you—there is perfection in you also,

You furnish your parts toward eternity,

Great or small, you furnish your parts toward the soul.

This poem is reminiscent of the work of the Transcendentalists (see "The Chambered Nautilus" by Oliver Wendell Holmes on p. 62)

A Noiseless Patient Spider

A noiseless patient spider,
I mark'd where on a little promontory it stood isolated,
Mark'd how to explore the vacant vast surrounding,
It launch'd forth filament, filament, filament, out of itself,
Ever unreeling them, ever tirelessly speeding them.

And you O my soul where you stand,
Surrounded, detached, in measureless oceans of space,
Ceaselessly musing, venturing, throwing, seeking the spheres to
    connect them,
Till the bridge you will need be form'd, till the ductile anchor hold,
Till the gossamer thread you fling catch somewhere, O my soul.

This celebration of a distinctly American spirit celebrates work songs and folk songs that spring directly from the singers, a wholly unpremeditated art that owes nothing to poets and songwriters.

I Hear America Singing

I hear America singing, the varied carols I hear;
Those of mechanics—each one singing his, as it should be, blithe
    and strong;
The carpenter singing his, as he measures his plank or beam,
The mason singing his, as he makes ready for work, or leaves off
    work;
The boatman singing what belongs to him in his boat—the deck-
    hand singing on the steamboat deck;
The shoemaker singing as he sits on his bench—the hatter singing
    as he stands;
The wood-cutter's song—the ploughboy's, on his way in the
    morning, or at the noon intermission, or at sundown;
The delicious singing of the mother—or of the young wife at work—
    or of the girl sewing or washing;
Each singing what belongs to her, and to none else;
The day what belongs to the day—at night, the party of young
    fellows, robust, friendly,
Singing, with open mouths, their strong melodious songs.

This is yet another of Whitman's tributes to a natural creativity that defies analysis, perhaps a criticism of the kind of academic poetry that his work rejects.

When I Heard the Learn'd Astronomer

When I heard the learn'd astronomer,
When the proofs, the figures, were ranged in columns before me,
When I was shown the charts and diagrams, to add, divide, and
    measure them,
When I sitting heard the astronomer where he lectured with much
    applause in the lecture-room,
How soon unaccountable I became tired and sick,
Till rising and gliding out I wander'd off by myself,
In the mystical moist night-air, and from time to time,
Look'd up in perfect silence at the stars.

The death of Lincoln provided Whitman with the occasion for a poem that combines all the motifs that characterize his work: a profoundly American spirit, a love of nature, a repudiation of artifice, and the deeply felt belief of an everlasting continuity of human endeavor and the human soul that transcends physical death.

When Lilacs Last in the Dooryard Bloom'd

1

When lilacs last in the dooryard bloom'd,
And the great star early droop'd in the western sky in the night,
I mourn'd, and yet shall mourn with ever-returning spring.
Ever-returning spring, trinity sure to me you bring,
Lilac blooming perennial and drooping star in the west,
And thought of him I love.

2

O powerful western fallen star!
O shades of night—O moody, tearful night!
O great star disappear'd—O the black murk that hides the star!
O cruel hands that hold me powerless—O helpless soul of me!
O harsh surrounding cloud that will not free my soul.

3

In the dooryard fronting an old farm-house near the white-wash'd
 palings,
Stands the lilac-bush tall-growing with heart-shaped leaves of rich
 green,
With many a pointed blossom rising delicate, with the perfume
 strong I love,
With every leaf a miracle—and from this bush in the dooryard,
With delicate-color'd blossoms and heart-shaped leaves of rich
 green,
A sprig with its flower I break.

4

In the swamp in secluded recesses,
A shy and hidden bird is warbling a song.

Solitary the thrush,
The hermit withdrawn to himself, avoiding the settlements,
Sings by himself a song.

Song of the bleeding throat,
Death's outlet song of life, (for well dear brother I know,
If thou wast not granted to sing, thou would'st surely die.)

5

Over the breast of the spring, the land, amid cities,
Amid lanes and through old woods, where lately the violets peep'd
    from the ground, spotting the gray debris,
Amid the grass in the fields each side of the lanes, passing the
    endless grass,
Passing the yellow-spear'd wheat, every grain from its shroud in the
    dark-brown fields uprisen,
Passing the apple-tree blows of white and pink in the orchards,
Carrying a corpse to where it shall rest in the grave,
Night and day journeys a coffin.

6

Coffin that passes through lanes and streets,
Through day and night with the great cloud darkening the land,
With the pomp of the inloop'd flags with the cities draped in black,
With the show of the States themselves as of crepe-veil'd women
    standing,
With processions long and winding and the flambeaus of the night,
With the countless torches lit, with the silent sea of faces and the
    unbared heads,
With the waiting depot, the arriving coffin, and the sombre faces,
With dirges through the night, with the thousand voices rising
    strong and solemn,
With all the mournful voices of the dirges pour'd around the coffin,
The dim-lit churches and the shuddering organs—where amid these
    you journey,
With the tolling bells' perpetual clang,
Here, coffin that slowly passes,
I give you a sprig of lilac.

7

(Nor for you, for one alone,
Blossoms and branches green to coffins all I bring,
For fresh as the morning, thus would I chant a song for you O sane
and sacred death.

All over bouquets of roses,
O death, I cover you with roses and early lilies,
But mostly and now the lilac that blooms the first,
Copious I break, I break the sprigs from the bushes,
With loaded arms I come, pouring for you,
For you and the coffins all of you, O death.)

8

O western orb sailing the heaven,
Now I know what you must have meant as a month since I walk'd,
As I walk'd in silence the transparent shadowy night,
As I saw you had something to tell as you bent to me night after
night,
As you droop'd from the sky low down as if to my side, (while the
other stars all look'd on,)
As we wander'd together the solemn night, (for something I know
not what kept me from sleep,)
As the night advanced, and I saw on the rim of the west how full
you were of woe,
As I stood on the rising ground in the breeze in the cool transparent
night,
As I watch'd where you pass'd and was lost in the netherward black
of the night,
As my soul in its trouble dissatisfied sank, as where you sad orb,
Concluded, dropt in the night, and was gone.

9

Sing on there in the swamp,
O singer bashful and tender, I hear your notes, I hear your call,
I hear, I come presently, I understand you,
But a moment I linger, for the lustrous star has detain'd me,
The star my departing comrade holds and detains me.

10

O how shall I warble myself for the dead one there I loved?
And how shall I deck my soul for the large sweet soul that has
    gone?
And what shall my perfume be for the grave of him I love?

Sea-winds blown from east and west,
Blown from the Eastern sea and blown from the Western sea, till
    there on the prairies meeting,
These and with these and the breath of my chant,
I'll perfume the grave of him I love.

11

O what shall I hang on the chamber walls?
And what shall the pictures be that I hang on the walls,
To adorn the burial-house of him I love?

Pictures of growing spring and farms and homes,
With the Fourth-month eve at sundown, and the gray smoke lucid
    and bright,
With floods of the yellow gold of the gorgeous, indolent, sinking sun,
    burning, expanding the air,

With the fresh sweet herbage under foot, and the pale green leaves
of the trees prolific,
In the distance of the flowing glaze, the breast of the river, with a
wind-dapple here and there,
With ranging hills on the banks, with many a line against the sky,
and shadows,
And the city at hand with dwellings so dense, and stacks of
chimneys,
And all the scenes of life and the workshops, and the workmen
homeward returning.

12

Lo, body and soul—this land,
My own Manhattan with spires, and the sparkling and hurrying
tides, and the ships,
The varied and ample land, the South and the North in the light,
Ohio's shores and flashing Missouri,
And ever the far-spreading prairies cover'd with grass and corn.

Lo, the most excellent sun so calm and haughty,
The violet and purple morn with just-felt breezes,
The gentle soft-born measureless light,
The miracle spreading bathing all, the fulfill'd noon,
The coming eve delicious, the welcome night and the stars,
Over my cities shining all, enveloping man and land.

13

Sing on, sing on, you gray-brown bird,
Sing from the swamps, the recesses, pour your chant from the
bushes,
Limitless out of the dusk, out of the cedars and pines.

Sing on dearest brother, warble your reedy song,
Loud human song, with voice of uttermost woe.

O liquid and free and tender!
O wild and loose to my soul—O wondrous singer!
You only I hear—yet the star holds me, (but will soon depart,)
Yet the lilac with mastering odor holds me.

14

Now while I sat in the day and look'd forth,
In the close of the day with its light and the fields of spring, and the
    farmers preparing their crops,
In the large unconscious scenery of my land with its lakes and
    forests,
In the heavenly aerial beauty, (after the perturb'd winds and storms,)
Under the arching heavens of the afternoon swift passing, and the
    voices of children and women,
The many-moving sea-tides, and I saw the ships how they sail'd,
And the summer approaching with richness, and the fields all busy
    with labor,
And the infinite separate houses, how they all went on, each with its
    meals and minutia of daily usages,
And the streets how their throbbings throbb'd, and the cities pent—
    lo, then and there,
Falling upon them all and among them all, enveloping me with the
    rest,
Appear'd the cloud, appear'd the long black trail,
And I knew death, its thought, and the sacred knowledge of death.
Then with the knowledge of death as walking one side of me,
And the thought of death close-walking the other side of me,
And I in the middle as with companions, and as holding the hands
    of companions,

I fled forth to the hiding receiving night that talks not,
Down to the shores of the water, the path by the swamp in the
   dimness,
To the solemn shadowy cedars and the ghostly pines so still.

And the singer so shy to the rest receiv'd me,
The gray-brown bird I know receiv'd us comrades three,
And he sang the carol of death, and a verse for him I love.

From deep secluded recesses,
From the fragrant cedars and the ghostly pines so still,
Came the carol of the bird.

And the charm of the carol rapt me,
As I held as if by their hands my comrades in the night,
And the voice of my spirit tallied the song of the bird.

Come lovely and soothing death,
Undulate round the world, serenely arriving, arriving,
In the day, in the night, to all, to each,
Sooner or later delicate death.

Prais'd be the fathomless universe,
For life and joy, and for objects and knowledge curious,
And for love, sweet love—but praise! praise! praise!
For the sure-enwinding arms of cool-enfolding death.

Dark mother always gliding near with soft feet,
Have none chanted for thee a chant of fullest welcome?
Then I chant it for thee, I glorify thee above all,
I bring thee a song that when thou must indeed come, come
   unfalteringly.

Approach strong deliveress,
When it is so, when thou hast taken them I joyously sing the dead,
Lost in the loving floating ocean of thee,
Laved in the flood of thy bliss, O death.

From me to thee glad serenades,
Dances for thee I propose saluting thee, adornments and feastings for thee,
And the sights of the open landscape and the high-spread sky are
*   fitting,*
And life and the fields, and the huge and thoughtful night.

The night in silence under many a star,
The ocean shore and the husky whispering wave whose voice I know,
And the soul turning to thee O vast and well-veil'd death,
And the body gratefully nestling close to thee.

Over the tree-tops I float thee a song,
Over the rising and sinking waves, over the myriad fields and the
*   prairies wide,*
Over the dense-pack'd cities and all the teeming wharves and ways,
I float this carol with joy, with joy to thee O death.

15

To the tally of my soul,
Loud and strong kept up the gray-brown bird,
With pure, deliberate notes, spreading, filling the night.

Loud in the pines and cedars dim,
Clear in the freshness moist and the swamp-perfume,
And I with my comrades there in the night.

While my sight that was bound in my eyes unclosed,
As to long panoramas of visions.

And I saw askant the armies,
I saw as in noiseless dreams hundreds of battle-flags,
Borne through the smoke of the battles and pierced with missiles I
  saw them,
And carried hither and yon through the smoke and torn and
  bloody,
And at last but a few shreds left on the staffs, (all in silence,)
And the staffs all splinter'd and broken.

I saw battle-corpses, myriads of them,
And the white skeletons of young men, I saw them,
I saw the debris and debris of all the dead soldiers of the war,
But I saw they were not as was thought,
They themselves were fully at rest, they suffer'd not,
The living remain'd and suffer'd, the mother suffer'd,
And the wife and the child and the musing comrade suffer'd,
And the armies that remain'd suffer'd.

16

Passing the visions, passing the night,
Passing, unloosing the hold of my comrades' hands,
Passing the song of the hermit bird and the tallying song of my soul,
Victorious song, death's outlet song, yet varying ever-altering song,
As low and wailing, yet clear the notes, rising and falling, flooding
  the night,
Sadly sinking and fainting, as warning and warning, and yet again
  bursting with joy,
Covering the earth and filling the spread of the heaven,
As that powerful psalm in the night I heard from recesses,

Passing, I leave thee lilac with heart-shaped leaves,
I leave thee there in the door-yard, blooming, returning with
 spring.

I cease from my song for thee,
From my gaze on thee in the west, fronting the west, communing
 with thee,
O comrade lustrous with silver face in the night.

Yet each to keep and all, retrievements out of the night,
The song, the wondrous chant of the gray-brown bird,
And the tallying chant, the echo arous'd in my soul,
With the lustrous and drooping star with the countenance full
 of woe,
With the holders holding my hand nearing the call of the bird,
Comrades mine and I in the midst, and their memory ever to keep
 for the dead I loved so well,
For the sweetest, wisest soul of all my days and lands—and this for
 his dear sake,
Lilac and star and bird twined with the chant of my soul,
There in the fragrant pines and the cedars dusk and dim.

JULIA WARD HOWE
(1819–1910)

Julia Ward Howe and her husband were prominent abolitionists who also worked to improve sanitary conditions in military camps and hospitals during the Civil War. Invited to the White House to meet with President Lincoln in 1862, the Howes visited a military camp across the Potomac River in Virginia, where they heard Union soldiers singing "John Brown's body lies a-mouldering in the grave." Someone suggested to Mrs. Howe, a published poet, that she write more suitable verses to the popular tune. According to her later account, "I went to bed and slept as usual, but awoke the next morning in the gray of the early dawn, and to my astonishment found that the wished-for lines were arranging themselves in my brain. I lay quite still until the last verse had completed itself in my thoughts, then hastily arose, saying to myself, I shall lose this if I don't write it down immediately. I searched for an old sheet of paper and an old stub of a pen which I had had the night before, and began to scrawl the lines almost without looking, as I learned to do by often scratching down verses in the darkened room when my little children were sleeping. Having completed this, I lay down again and fell asleep, but not before feeling that something of importance had happened to me." Her poem was soon published in the *Atlantic Monthly* and became an instant success. With its conflation of the antislavery cause with God's will, it transcends political issues like states rights and preservation of the Union often referred to as causes for the conflict, and grounds it forever as a war fought to make all Americans free.

Battle-Hymn of the Republic

Mine eyes have seen the glory of the coming of the Lord:
He is trampling out the vintage where the grapes of wrath are stored;
He hath loosed the fateful lightning of His terrible swift sword:
　　His truth is marching on.

Chorus
Glory! Glory! Hallelujah!
Glory! Glory! Hallelujah!
Glory! Glory! Hallelujah!
His truth is marching on.

I have seen Him in the watch-fires of a hundred circling camps;
They have builded Him an altar in the evening dews and damps;
I can read His righteous sentence by the dim and flaring lamps.
　　His day is marching on.

Chorus

I have read a fiery gospel, writ in burnished rows of steel:
"As ye deal with my condemners, so with you my grace shall deal";
Let the Hero, born of woman, crush the serpent with his heel,
　　Since God is marching on."

Chorus

He has sounded forth the trumpet that shall never call retreat;
He is sifting out the hearts of men before his judgment-seat:
Oh! be swift, my soul, to answer Him! be jubilant, my feet!
　　Our God is marching on.

Chorus

In the beauty of the lilies Christ was born across the sea,
With a glory in his bosom that transfigures you and me:
As He died to make men holy, let us die to make men free,
    While God is marching on.

Chorus

The traditional Negro spiritual often applied biblically inspired imagery to the lives and aspirations of the people singing the songs. Freedom is a constant theme, though sometimes expressed in the sense of resurrection, as in "Swing Low, Sweet Chariot." But there can be no more direct connection to the lives of American slaves than the one made in the version of "Go Down, Moses," appearing below.

Go Down, Moses

Go down, Moses,
Way down in Egyptland
Tell old Pharaoh,
To let my people go.

When Israel was in Egyptland
Let my people go
Oppressed so hard they could not stand
Let my people go.

Go down, Moses,
Way down in Egyptland
Tell old Pharaoh,
"Let my people go."

"Thus saith the Lord," bold Moses said,
"Let my people go;
If not, I'll smite your first-born dead
Let my people go.

"No more shall they in bondage toil,
Let my people go;
Let them come out with Egypt's spoil,
Let my people go."

The Lord told Moses what to do,
Let my people go;
To lead the children of Israel through,
Let my people go.

Go down, Moses,
Way down in Egyptland
Tell old Pharaoh,
Let my people go.

This is not a proper spiritual, but rather a type of puzzle song, supposedly used by Southern slaves as a guide northward to freedom. The "drinking gourd" is a reference to the constellation of the Big Dipper, the handle of which always points north; other references are directional clues to landmarks along the way.

Follow the Drinking Gourd

When the Sun comes back
And the first quail calls
Follow the Drinking Gourd,
For the old man is a-waiting for to carry you to freedom
If you follow the Drinking Gourd.

The riverbank makes a very good road.
The dead trees will show you the way.
Left foot, peg foot, travelling on,
Follow the Drinking Gourd.

The river ends between two hills
Follow the Drinking Gourd.
There's another river on the other side
Follow the Drinking Gourd.

When the great big river meets the little river
Follow the Drinking Gourd.
For the old man is a-waiting for to carry you to freedom
If you follow the Drinking Gourd.

STEPHEN C. FOSTER

(1826–1864)

The lyric form has been a prominent feature of English poetry for centuries, from Ben Jonson's "To Celia" ("Drink to me only with thine eyes"), to John Donne's "Go, and Catch a Falling Star," Lord Byron's "She Walks in Beauty," and countless others. While Stephen Foster is celebrated as the progenitor of the American popular song, he can also be credited with establishing a standard for the American lyric poem with such works as "Beautiful Dreamer" and the verses below.

Jeanie with the Light Brown Hair

I dream of Jeanie with the light brown hair,
Borne, like a zephyr, on the summer air;
I see her tripping where the bright streams play,
Happy as the daisies that dance on her way.

Many were the wild notes her merry voice would pour,
Many were the blithe birds that warbled them o'er:
Oh! I dream of Jeanie with the light brown hair,
Floating, like a zephyr, on the soft summer air.

I long for Jeanie with the day dawn smile,
Radiant in gladness, warm with winning guile;
I hear her melodies, like joys gone by,
Sighing 'round my heart o'er the fond hopes that die:

Sighing like the night wind and sobbing like the rain,
Wailing for the lost one that comes not again:
Oh! I long for Jeanie and my heart bows low,
Never more to find her where the bright waters flow.

I sigh for Jeanie, but her light form strayed
Far from the fond hearts 'round her native glade;
Her smiles have vanished and her sweet songs flown,
Flitting like the dreams that have cheered us and gone.

Now the nodding wild flow'rs may wither on the shore
While her gentle fingers will cull them no more:
Oh! I sigh for Jeanie with the light brown hair,
Floating, like a zephyr, on the soft summer air.

Writers like Foster often created works designed to be sung in minstrel shows, by white performers in blackface makeup. But Foster himself, born in Pittsburgh and raised in the North, wrote songs that did not ridicule or debase the slaves of his time, as many other minstrel songs did (he himself preferred the term "plantation songs"). Rather he humanized his subjects, and found in their yearnings a commonality of interest with people everywhere, so much so that his songs were later praised for their humanity by notable African Americans such as W. C. Handy and W. E. B. DuBois.

The "Swanee River" referred to in the lyrics is a contraction of the Suwanee River in Florida; the longer version of the name did not fit the meter of the song.

Old Folks at Home

Way down upon the Swanee River,
Far, far away—
That's where my heart is turning ever,
That's where the old folks stay.
All up and down the whole creation,
Sadly I roam.
Still longing for the old plantation,
And for the old folks at home.

All the world is sad and dreary, everywhere I roam.
Oh darkies, how my heart grows weary
Far from the old folks at home.

All 'round the little farm I wandered,
When I was young.
Then many happy days I squandered,
Many the songs I sung.
When I was playing with my brother,
Happy was I.
Oh, take me to my kind old mother,
There let me live and die.

All the world is sad and dreary, everywhere I roam.
Oh darkies, how my heart grows weary
Far from the old folks at home.

One little hut among the bushes,
One that I love
Still sadly to my mem'ry rushes,
No matter where I rove.
When shall I see the bees a humming,
All 'round the comb?
When shall I hear the banjo strumming,
Down by my good old home?

All the world is sad and dreary, everywhere I roam.
Oh darkies, how my heart grows weary,
Far from the old folks at home.

EMILY DICKINSON
(1830–1886)

Emily Dickinson lived a reclusive life, which has left room for much speculation about the nature of the connections she had with her numerous friends and family, along with questions about her inner life and personal philosophy. She was apparently a brilliant student, yet returned home before completing college and effectively never left again, though she maintained a wide correspondence and numerous close relationships, and often served as her father's hostess when he entertained. She wrote hundreds of poems, yet, though a few appeared in the *Atlantic Monthly,* most of her work, written in her hand and bound with thread in small booklets, remained unpublished during her life. Only after Dickinson's death were her verses brought before the public, largely through the efforts of one of her early friends and supporters, Thomas Wentworth Higginson, the editor of the *Atlantic Monthly.* Dickinson's poetry met with general approbation, though one noted critic of the day, Thomas Bailey Aldrich, denigrated her work in the same magazine, asserting that "the incoherence and formlessness of her versicles are fatal." Of course it's often difficult to recognize greatness when it is expressed in a form different from any known before. What Aldrich saw as incoherence and formlessness we now appreciate as acute insights and images that can pierce a reader to the soul.

Most of Dickinson's poems were written without conventional punctuation, with the lines set off by dashes, as in the first poem below. Usually, though, they are rendered in more traditional form, as in the rest of the poems appearing here.

Wild nights!—wild nights!

Wild nights—wild nights!
Were I with thee,
Wild Nights should be
Our luxury!

Futile the winds
To a heart in port—
Done with the compass,
Done with the chart!

Rowing in Eden—
Ah! the sea!
Might I moor, tonight,
In thee!

This poem, often found in schoolbooks, is not just a paean to the joys of reading, but a tribute to the capacity of the soul to extend beyond the physical limitations of the body, a significant statement from this reclusive poet.

There is no frigate like a book

There is no frigate like a book
To take us lands away,
Nor any coursers like a page
Of prancing poetry.
This traverse may the poorest take
Without oppress of toll;
How frugal is the chariot
That bears a human soul!

This poem contains one of Dickinson's most striking and memorable images.

"Hope" is the thing with feathers

"Hope" is the thing with feathers
That perches in the soul
And sings the tune without the words
And never stops at all,

And sweetest in the gale is heard;
And sore must be the storm
That could abash the little bird
That kept so many warm.

I've heard it in the chillest land
And on the strangest sea,
Yet never, in extremity,
It asked a crumb of me.

Dickinson may have enjoyed a glass of wine occasionally, but the liquor
of this poem is the sweet fresh air of a summer morning. Her expression
of the joy and significance of Nature is markedly distinct from the more
portentous writings of the Transcendentalists.

I taste a liquor never brewed

I taste a liquor never brewed,
From tankards scooped in pearl;
Not all the vats upon the Rhine
Yield such an alcohol!

Inebriate of air am I,
And debauchee of dew,
Reeling, through endless summer days,
From inns of molten blue.

When landlords turn the drunken bee
Out of the foxglove's door,
When butterflies renounce their drams,
I shall but drink the more!

Till seraphs swing their snowy hats,
And saints to windows run,
To see the little tippler
Leaning against the sun!

The tone of this poem is almost childlike, but the second verse reveals a dryly witty and completely sophisticated barb.

I'm nobody! Who are you?

I'm nobody! Who are you?
Are you nobody, too?
Then there's a pair of us—don't tell!
They'd banish us, you know.

How dreary to be somebody!
How public, like a frog
To tell your name the livelong day
To an admiring bog!

It's been often noted that much of Emily Dickinson's poetry is written in the same meter as the popular song "The Yellow Rose of Texas."

Because I could not stop for Death

Because I could not stop for Death,
He kindly stopped for me;
The carriage held but just ourselves
And Immortality.

We slowly drove, he knew no haste,
And I had put away
My labor, and my leisure too,
For his civility.

We passed the school where children played
At wrestling in a ring;
We passed the fields of gazing grain,
We passed the setting sun.

We paused before a house that seemed
A swelling of the ground;
The roof was scarcely visible,
The cornice but a mound.

Since then 'tis centuries; but each
Feels shorter than the day
I first surmised the horses' heads
Were toward eternity.

HUGH ANTOINE D'ARCY

(1843–1925)

Supposedly d'Arcy, a journalist, wrote this poem about a derelict drunk he picked up from the steps of Joe Smith's Barroom in Union Square in New York City in 1877. The poem achieved wide popularity in its day, and was often declaimed from the stage. Today we can see it as an early example of the tone of sentimental melodrama that permeates much of contemporary American popular culture.

The Face on the Barroom Floor

'Twas a balmy summer evening, and a goodly crowd was there,
Which well-nigh filled Joe's barroom, on the corner of the square;
And as songs and witty stories came through the open door,
A vagabond crept slowly in and posed upon the floor.

"Where did it come from?" someone said. "The wind has blown
    it in."
"What does it want?" another cried. "Some whiskey, rum or gin?"
"Here, Toby, sic 'em, if your stomach's equal to the work—
I wouldn't touch him with a fork, he's filthy as a Turk."

This badinage the poor wretch took with stoical good grace;
In fact, he smiled as tho' he thought he'd struck the proper place.
"Come, boys, I know there's kindly hearts among so good a
    crowd—
To be in such good company would make a deacon proud.

"Give me a drink—that's what I want—I'm out of funds, you know,
When I had cash to treat the gang this hand was never slow.
What? You laugh as if you thought this pocket never held a sou;
I once was fixed as well, my boys, as any one of you.

"There, thanks, that's braced me nicely; God bless you one and all;
Next time I pass this good saloon I'll make another call.
Give you a song? No, I can't do that; my singing days are past;
My voice is cracked, my throat's worn out, and my lungs are going
    fast.

"I'll tell you a funny story, and a fact, I promise, too.
Say! Give me another whiskey, and I'll tell what I'll do—
That I was ever a decent man not one of you would think;
But I was, some four or five years back. Say, give me another drink.

"Fill her up, Joe, I want to put some life into my frame—
Such little drinks to a bum like me are miserably tame;
Five fingers—there, that's the scheme—and corking whiskey, too.
Well, here's luck, boys, and landlord, my best regards to you.

"You've treated me pretty kindly and I'd like to tell you how
I came to be the dirty sot you see before you now.
As I told you, once I was a man, with muscle, frame, and health,
And but for a blunder ought to have made considerable wealth.

"I was a painter—not one that daubed on bricks and wood,
But an artist, and for my age, was rated pretty good.
I worked hard at my canvas, and was bidding fair to rise,
For gradually I saw the star of fame before my eyes.

"I made a picture perhaps you've seen, 'tis called the 'Chase of
    Fame.'
It brought me fifteen hundred pounds and added to my name,
And then I met a woman—now comes the funny part—
With eyes that petrified my brain, and sunk into my heart.

"Why don't you laugh? 'Tis funny that the vagabond you see
Could ever love a woman, and expect her love for me;
But 'twas so, and for a month or two, her smiles were freely given,
And when her loving lips touched mine, it carried me to Heaven.

"Boys, did you ever see a girl for whom your soul you'd give,
With a form like the Milo Venus, too beautiful to live;
With eyes that would beat the Koh-i-noor, and a wealth of chestnut
    hair?
If so, 'twas she, for there never was another half so fair.

"I was working on a portrait, one afternoon in May,
Of a fair-haired boy, a friend of mine, who lived across the way.
And Madeline admired it, and much to my surprise,
Said she'd like to know the man that had such dreamy eyes.

"It didn't take long to know him, and before the month had flown
My friend had stole my darling, and I was left alone;
And ere a year of misery had passed above my head,
The jewel I had treasured so had tarnished and was dead.

"That's why I took to drink, boys. Why, I never see you smile,
I thought you'd be amused, and laughing all the while.
Why, what's the matter, friend? There's a tear-drop in your eye,
Come, laugh like me. 'Tis only babes and women that should cry.

"Say, boys, if you give me just another whiskey I'll be glad,
And I'll draw right here a picture of the face that drove me mad.
Give me that piece of chalk with which you mark the baseball
    score—
You shall see the lovely Madeline upon the barroom floor."

Another drink, and with chalk in hand, the vagabond began
To sketch a face that well might buy the soul of any man.
Then, as he placed another lock upon the shapely head,
With a fearful shriek, he leaped and fell across the picture—dead.

TRADITIONAL WESTERN SONG
(LATE NINETEENTH CENTURY)

The familiar image of the cowboy remains an essential component of American popular culture. The cowboys of the late nineteenth century were generally members of gangs of hired hands recruited to help brand and drive herds of cattle to feed in the open ranges of Wyoming, Idaho, or Montana and then to railheads in Kansas, from where they could be transported to major urban areas for slaughter. Somehow this harsh existence became romanticized into a life of freedom and nobility, doubtless helped in some measure by the popularity of lyrics like the ones below. Ostensibly once sung by cowboys to pass the time and lull the cattle, this song, rooted in British balladry, has been transformed by the folk process into classic Americana.

Git Along, Little Dogies

As I was walkin' one mornin' for pleasure,
I spied a cowpuncher a-ridin along.
His hat was throwed back and his spurs were a-jingling,
And as he approached, he was singin' this song:

Chorus
Whoopie-ti-yi-yo, get along little dogies,
It's your misfortune and none of my own.
Whoopie-ti-yi-yo, get along little dogies
You know that Wyoming will be your new home.

It's early in the spring when we round up the dogies,
We mark 'em and brand 'em and bob off their tails.
We round up the horses, load up the chuck-wagon,
Then send the dogies out on the long trail.

Chorus

Your mother was raised away down in Texas,
Where the jimson weed and the 'sanders grow
We'll feed you up on prickly-pear and choya
And then send you lopin' to old Idaho.

Chorus

TRANSLATED BY JAMES MOONEY

(CA. 1890)

By the late 1880s the centuries-old culture of the Indians of the American plains had been effectively destroyed, largely through indiscriminate slaughter of their primary food source, the buffalo (or American bison). The efforts of missionaries to bring Christianity to the Indians took an unexpected turn when a Paiute named Wovoka became convinced that he was the Messiah, and would help lead the Indians to a new golden age, in which the white men would disappear and the buffalo would return. This new belief was transmitted to various tribes of the Great Plains through the Ghost Dance, in which tribespeople (often women, since so many of the men had died in the wars against the U.S. Army that preceded this period) danced to exhaustion. By the time the Ghost Dance reached the Lakota Sioux, the legend had become extended to the point that believers now wore Ghost Shirts, which they were told would protect them from the army's bullets. The movement came to a tragic end with the so-called "Battle" of Wounded Knee in late 1890, in which over a hundred men, women, and children were killed. Subsequently twenty Congressional Medals of Honor were awarded to army combatants in the incident, the largest number ever awarded for a single engagement.

Sioux Ghost Dance

The whole world is coming.
A nation is coming, a nation is coming,
The Eagle has brought the message to the tribe.
The father says so, the father says so.
Over the whole earth they are coming.
The buffalo are coming, the buffalo are coming,
The Crow has brought the message to the tribe,
The father says so, the father says so.

EMMA LAZARUS

(1849–1887)

Liberty Enlightening the World, as the Statue of Liberty was originally called, was a gift to the United States from France to mark the hundredth anniversary of U.S. independence in 1876 (and the French alliance with the Colonial government that made that independence possible). But while the statue was a gift, the cost of the pedestal was to be the responsibility of the American people. Emma Lazarus's poem was written as a contribution to the fundraising effort, and was preserved on a plaque that was placed on the pedestal in 1903. The sculptor, Frédéric Auguste Bartholdi, intended that the statue not only commemorate the alliance between France and the United States at the time of the American Revolution, but also help inspire European nations to build freer societies. Instead, as the poem indicates, the statue inspired the oppressed of Europe to seek liberty in America, guided by the statue's lamp.

The New Colossus

Not like the brazen giant of Greek fame,
With conquering limbs astride from land to land;
Here at our sea-washed, sunset gates shall stand
A mighty woman with a torch, whose flame
Is the imprisoned lightning, and her name
Mother of Exiles. From her beacon-hand
Glows world-wide welcome; her mild eyes command
The air-bridged harbor that twin cities frame,
"Keep, ancient lands, your storied pomp!" cries she
With silent lips. "Give me your tired, your poor,
Your huddled masses yearning to breathe free,
The wretched refuse of your teeming shore,
Send these, the homeless, tempest-tost to me,
I lift my lamp beside the golden door!"

EUGENE FIELD

(1850–1895)

During his life Field was an immensely popular newspaper columnist and poet. The poem below, written in memory of one of his own children, is sentimental to the point of mawkishness, but the essential honesty of the emotions expressed has insured its timelessness.

Little Boy Blue

The little toy dog is covered with dust,
    But sturdy and stanch he stands;
And the little toy soldier is red with rust,
    And his musket moulds in his hands.
Time was when the little toy dog was new,
    And the soldier was passing fair;
And that was the time when our Little Boy Blue
    Kissed them and put them there.

"Now, don't you go till I come," he said,
    "And don't you make any noise!"
So, toddling off to his trundle bed,
    He dreamt of the pretty toys;
And, as he was dreaming, an angel song
    Awakened our Little Boy Blue—
Oh! the years are many, the years are long,
    But the little toy friends are true!

Ay, faithful to Little Boy Blue they stand,
  Each in the same old place,
Awaiting the touch of a little hand,
  The smile of a little face;
And they wonder, as waiting the long years through
  In the dust of that little chair,
What has become of our Little Boy Blue,
  Since he kissed them and put them there.

ERNEST THAYER
(1863–1940)

Ernest Thayer was a college friend of William Randolph Hearst, and when Hearst took over management of his father's newspaper the *San Francisco Examiner,* Thayer joined him as a humor columnist, using the pen name of Phin. On June 3, 1888, the poem that was to become known as "Casey at the Bat" was published anonymously in the *Examiner.* It remained unknown until a well-known stage performer named DeWolf Hopper was handed a clipping of the poem with the suggestion that he recite it before an audience including members of the New York and Chicago major league teams. The poem became an instant sensation (Hopper later claimed to have performed the poem over ten thousand times), and its mock-heroic style—almost Homeric in its tone—remains as readable today as it was over a century ago.

Casey at the Bat
A Ballad of the Republic, Sung in the Year 1888

The outlook wasn't brilliant for the Mudville nine that day:
The score stood four to two, with but one inning more to play,
And then when Cooney died at first, and Barrows did the same,
A pall-like silence fell upon the patrons of the game.

A straggling few got up to go in deep despair. The rest
Clung to that hope which springs eternal in the human breast;
They thought, "If only Casey could but get a whack at that—
We'd put up even money now, with Casey at the bat."

But Flynn preceded Casey, as did also Jimmy Blake,
And the former was a hoodoo, and the latter was a cake;
So upon that stricken multitude grim melancholy sat,
For there seemed but little chance of Casey's getting to the bat.

But Flynn let drive a single, to the wonderment of all,
And Blake, the much despisèd, tore the cover off the ball;
And when the dust had lifted, and the men saw what had occurred,
There was Jimmy safe at second and Flynn a-hugging third.

Then from five thousand throats and more there rose a lusty yell;
It rumbled through the valley, it rattled in the dell;
It pounded on the mountain and recoiled upon the flat,
For Casey, mighty Casey, was advancing to the bat.

There was ease in Casey's manner as he stepped into his place;
There was pride in Casey's bearing and a smile on Casey's face.
And when, responding to the cheers, he lightly doffed his hat,
No stranger in the crowd could doubt 'twas Casey at the bat.

Ten thousand eyes were on him as he rubbed his hands with dirt;
Five thousand tongues applauded when he wiped them on his shirt;
Then while the writhing pitcher ground the ball into his hip,
Defiance flashed in Casey's eye, a sneer curled Casey's lip.

And now the leather-covered sphere came hurtling through the air,
And Casey stood a-watching it in haughty grandeur there.
Close by the sturdy batsman the ball unheeded sped—
"That ain't my style," said Casey. "Strike one," the umpire said.

From the benches, black with people, there went up a muffled roar,
Like the beating of the storm-waves on a stern and distant shore;
"Kill him! Kill the umpire!" shouted some one on the stand;
And it's likely they'd have killed him had not Casey raised his hand.

With a smile of Christian charity great Casey's visage shone;
He stilled the rising tumult; he bade the game go on;
He signaled to the pitcher, and once more the dun sphere flew;
But Casey still ignored it, and the umpire said, "Strike two."

"Fraud!" cried the maddened thousands, and echo answered
    "Fraud!"
But one scornful look from Casey and the audience was awed.
They saw his face grow stern and cold, they saw his muscles strain,
And they knew that Casey wouldn't let that ball go by again.

The sneer is gone from Casey's lip, his teeth are clenched in hate;
He pounds with cruel violence his bat upon the plate.
And now the pitcher holds the ball, and now he lets it go,
And now the air is shattered by the force of Casey's blow.

Oh, somewhere in this favored land the sun is shining bright;
The band is playing somewhere, and somewhere hearts are light,
And somewhere men are laughing, and little children shout;
But there is no joy in Mudville—mighty Casey has struck out.

EDWIN ARLINGTON ROBINSON
(1869–1935)

Robinson described this poem as "a nice little thing....There isn't any idealism in it, but there's lots of something else—humanity, maybe." Of course the poem's last two lines provide an ironic commentary to the rest of the poem, but if the shock of the ending were the only significant quality of the work, it would be read once and then forgotten. Actually, the drama of the poem is found in the way the poet balances the envy of those observing Cory with the dark reality of his inner life that leads to his self-destruction. The essence of the poem can be expressed in Thoreau's famous aphorism that "The mass of men lead lives of quiet desperation."

Richard Cory

Whenever Richard Cory went down town,
We people on the pavement looked at him:
He was a gentleman from sole to crown,
Clean favored, and imperially slim.

And he was always quietly arrayed,
And he was always human when he talked;
But still he fluttered pulses when he said,
"Good Morning!" and he glittered when he walked.

And he was rich—yes, richer than a king—
And admirably schooled in every grace:
In fine, we thought that he was everything
To make us wish that we were in his place.

So on we worked and waited for the light,
And went without the meat, and cursed the bread;
And Richard Cory, one calm summer night,
Went home and put a bullet in his head.

EDGAR LEE MASTERS
(1869–1950)

Masters published the 244 poems that make up *Spoon River Anthology* in serial form between 1914 and 1915. Each poem is a free verse, first-person statement from one of the people ostensibly buried in the town's cemetery. Many of the speakers were in fact actual inhabitants of the area, including Anne Rutledge, who was long supposed to have had an emotional relationship with Abraham Lincoln during his time in Springfield, Illinois, although no objective evidence to this effect has ever been found.

Anne Rutledge from *Spoon River Anthology*

Out of me unworthy and unknown
The vibrations of deathless music;
"With malice toward none, with charity for all."
Out of me the forgiveness of millions toward millions,
And the beneficent face of a nation
Shining with justice and truth.
I am Anne Rutledge who sleep beneath these weeds,
Beloved in life of Abraham Lincoln,
Wedded to him, not through union,
But through separation.
Bloom forever, O Republic,
From the dust of my bosom!

STEPHEN CRANE

(1871–1900)

Stephen Crane might reasonably be called the anti-Whitman. Instead of rolling, biblical addresses to himself, humanity, and the world at large, Crane offers epigrammatic, ironic examples of the human propensity for self-delusion in verses that are virtually brief prose poems. In his cool, detached amusement, barely masking a fundamental despair, he is perhaps the first twentieth-century American poet. Sadly, this gifted writer died at the dawning of that century, leaving behind arguably the greatest war novel ever written (*The Red Badge of Courage*) along with these and other similar koan-like poems.

It's interesting to contrast the tone of this poem with Whitman's "When I Heard the Learn'd Astronomer" (p. 106).

A Man Said to the Universe

A man said to the universe:
"Sir I exist!"
"However," replied the universe,
"The fact has not created in me
A sense of obligation."

The stark imagery of this poem recalls the dreamlike horrors of Francisco Goya's famous series of etchings entitled *Nightmares*.

In the Desert
(from The Black Riders and Other Lines)

In the desert
I saw a creature, naked, bestial,
Who, squatting upon the ground,
Held his heart in his hands,
And ate of it.
I said, "Is it good, friend?"
"It is bitter—bitter," he answered;
"But I like it
Because it is bitter,
And because it is my heart."

ROBERT W. SERVICE

(1874–1958)

Robert Service was born in England, raised in Scotland, and wrote most often of the Canadian Yukon Territory, yet in his love of exaggerated narrative in a wilderness background he wrote in the great tradition of the American tall tale. Service did spend a short part of his life in Southern California, and even made a brief appearance in the 1942 film *The Spoilers,* starring John Wayne and Marlene Dietrich, which, according to its advertising, was about "Crashing Fists in the Gold-Crazed Alaska of '98."

Apparently Service once heard the name Sam McGee while working at a bank, and kept it in mind for future use in a poem.

The Cremation of Sam McGee

There are strange things done in the midnight sun
By the men who moil for gold;
The Arctic trails have their secret tales
That would make your blood run cold;
The Northern Lights have seen queer sights,
But the queerest they ever did see
Was that night on the marge of Lake Lebarge
I cremated Sam McGee.

Now Sam McGee was from Tennessee, where the cotton blooms
and blows.
Why he left his home in the South to roam 'round the Pole, God
only knows.
He was always cold, but the land of gold seemed to hold him like
a spell;
Though he'd often say in his homely way that he'd "sooner live in
hell."

On a Christmas Day we were mushing our way over the Dawson
trail.
Talk of your cold! through the parka's fold it stabbed like a driven
nail.
If our eyes we'd close, then the lashes froze till sometimes we
couldn't see;
It wasn't much fun, but the only one to whimper was Sam McGee.

And that very night, as we lay packed tight in our robes beneath the
snow,
And the dogs were fed, and the stars o'erhead were dancing heel
and toe,
He turned to me, and "Cap," says he, "I'll cash in this trip,
I guess;
And if I do, I'm asking that you won't refuse my last request."

Well, he seemed so low that I couldn't say no; then he says with a
sort of moan:
"It's the cursèd cold, and it's got right hold till I'm chilled clean
through to the bone.
Yet 'tain't being dead—it's my awful dread of the icy grave that
pains;
So I want you to swear that, foul or fair, you'll cremate my last
remains."

A pal's last need is a thing to heed, so I swore I would not fail;
And we started on at the streak of dawn; but God! he looked ghastly
pale.
He crouched on the sleigh, and he raved all day of his home in
Tennessee;
And before nightfall a corpse was all that was left of Sam McGee.

There wasn't a breath in that land of death, and I hurried, horror-
driven,
With a corpse half hid that I couldn't get rid, because of a promise
given;
It was lashed to the sleigh, and it seemed to say: "You may tax your
brawn and brains,
But you promised true, and it's up to you to cremate those last
remains."

Now a promise made is a debt unpaid, and the trail has its own stern
code.
In the days to come, though my lips were dumb, in my heart how I
cursed that load.
In the long, long night, by the lone firelight, while the huskies, round
in a ring,
Howled out their woes to the homeless snows—O God! how I
loathed the thing.

And every day that quiet clay seemed to heavy and heavier grow;
And on I went, though the dogs were spent and the grub was getting
low;
The trail was bad, and I felt half mad, but I swore I would not
give in;
And I'd often sing to the hateful thing, and it hearkened with
a grin.

Till I came to the marge of Lake Lebarge, and a derelict there lay;

It was jammed in the ice, but I saw in a trice it was called the "Alice May."

And I looked at it, and I thought a bit, and I looked at my frozen chum;

Then "Here," said I, with a sudden cry, "is my cre-ma-tor-eum."

Some planks I tore from the cabin floor, and I lit the boiler fire;

Some coal I found that was lying around, and I heaped the fuel higher;

The flames just soared, and the furnace roared—such a blaze you seldom see;

And I burrowed a hole in the glowing coal, and I stuffed in Sam McGee.

Then I made a hike, for I didn't like to hear him sizzle so;

And the heavens scowled, and the huskies howled, and the wind began to blow.

It was icy cold, but the hot sweat rolled down my cheeks, and I don't know why;

And the greasy smoke in an inky cloak went streaking down the sky.

I do not know how long in the snow I wrestled with grisly fear;

But the stars came out and they danced about ere again I ventured near;

I was sick with dread, but I bravely said: "I'll just take a peep inside.

I guess he's cooked, and it's time I looked"; . . . then the door I opened wide.

And there sat Sam, looking cool and calm, in the heart of the
   furnace roar;
And he wore a smile you could see a mile, and he said: "Please close
   that door.
It's fine in here, but I greatly fear you'll let in the cold and storm—
Since I left Plumtree, down in Tennessee, it's the first time I've been
   warm."

There are strange things done in the midnight sun
   By the men who moil for gold;
The Arctic trails have their secret tales
   That would make your blood run cold;
The Northern Lights have seen queer sights,
   But the queerest they ever did see
Was that night on the marge of Lake Lebarge
   I cremated Sam McGee.

While working as a newspaperman in White Horse in the Yukon, Service gained a reputation for reciting poetry, including "The Face on the Barroom Floor," causing his editor to suggest that he write his own poetry. One day, walking home from the newspaper office, Service heard loud noise from a neighboring saloon. According to legend, the thought occurred to him that a bunch of the boys were whooping it up that night, and the rest of this famous work soon followed.

The Shooting of Dan McGrew

A bunch of the boys were whooping it up in the Malamute saloon;
The kid that handles the music-box was hitting a jag-time tune;
Back of the bar, in a solo game, sat Dangerous Dan McGrew,
And watching his luck was his light-o'-love, the lady that's known
  as Lou.

When out of the night, which was fifty below, and into the din and
  glare,
There stumbled a miner fresh from the creeks, dog-dirty, and loaded
  for bear.
He looked like a man with a foot in the grave and scarcely the
  strength of a louse,
Yet he tilted a poke of dust on the bar, and he called for drinks for
  the house.
There was none could place the stranger's face, though we searched
  ourselves for a clue;
But we drank his health, and the last to drink was Dangerous Dan
  McGrew.

There's men that somehow just grip your eyes, and hold them hard like a spell;
And such was he, and he looked to me like a man who had lived in hell;
With a face most hair, and the dreary stare of a dog whose day is done,
As he watered the green stuff in his glass, and the drops fell one by one.
Then I got to figgering who he was, and wondering what he'd do,
And I turned my head—and there watching him was the lady that's known as Lou.

His eyes went rubbering round the room, and he seemed in a kind of daze,
Till at last that old piano fell in the way of his wandering gaze.
The rag-time kid was having a drink; there was no one else on the stool,
So the stranger stumbles across the room, and flops down there like a fool.
In a buckskin shirt that was glazed with dirt he sat, and I saw him sway;
Then he clutched the keys with his talon hands—my God! but that man could play.

Were you ever out in the Great Alone, when the moon was awful clear,
And the icy mountains hemmed you in with a silence you most could *hear*;
With only the howl of a timber wolf, and you camped there in the cold,
A half-dead thing in a stark, dead world, clean mad for the muck called gold;

While high overhead, green, yellow and red, the North Lights swept
in bars?—
Then you've a hunch what the music meant . . . hunger and might
and the stars.

And hunger not of the belly kind, that's banished with bacon and
beans,
But the gnawing hunger of lonely men for a home and all that it
means;
For a fireside far from the cares that are, four walls and a roof
above;
But oh! so cramful of cosy joy, and crowded with a woman's love—
A woman dearer than all the world, and true as Heaven is true—
(God! how ghastly she looks through her rouge,—the lady that's
known as Lou.)

Then on a sudden the music changed, so soft that you scarce could
hear;
But you felt that your life had been looted clean of all that it once
held dear;
That someone had stolen the woman you loved; that her love was a
devil's lie;
That your guts were gone, and the best for you was to crawl away
and die.
'Twas the crowning cry of a heart's despair, and it thrilled you
through and through—
"I guess I'll make it a spread misere," said Dangerous Dan McGrew.

The music almost dies away . . . then it burst like a pent-up flood;
And it seemed to say, "Repay, repay," and my eyes were blind with
blood.
The thought came back of an ancient wrong, and it stung like a
frozen lash,

And the lust awoke to kill, to kill . . . then the music stopped with a
    crash,
And the stranger turned, and his eyes they burned in a most peculiar
    way;

In a buckskin shirt that was glazed with dirt he sat, and I saw him
    sway;
Then his lips went in in a kind of grin, and he spoke, and his voice
    was calm,
And "Boys," says he, "you don't know me, and none of you care a
    damn;
But I want to state, and my words are straight, and I'll bet my poke
    they're true,
That one of you is a hound of hell . . . and that one is Dan
    McGrew."

Then I ducked my head and the lights went out, and two guns
    blazed in the dark;
And a woman screamed, and the lights went up, and two men lay
    stiff and stark.
Pitched on his head, and pumped full of lead, was Dangerous Dan
    McGrew,
While the man from the creeks lay clutched to the breast of the lady
    that's known as Lou.

These are the simple facts of the case, and I guess I ought to know.
They say that the stranger was crazed with "hooch," and I'm not
    denying it's so.
I'm not so wise as the lawyer guys, but strictly between us two—
The woman that kissed him and—pinched his poke—was the lady
    that's known as Lou.

164

JAMES WELDON JOHNSON

(1871–1938)

Originally written as a poem to be read at a celebration of Abraham Lincoln's birthday by students at the school in Jacksonville, Florida, where Johnson was principal, this work was set to music by Johnson's brother and adopted by the NAACP as the Negro National Anthem in 1919.

Lift Every Voice and Sing

Lift ev'ry voice and sing,
Till earth and heaven ring,
Ring with the harmonies of Liberty;
Let our rejoicing rise
High as the listening skies,
Let it resound loud as the rolling sea.
Sing a song full of the faith that the dark past has taught us,
Sing a song full of the hope that the present has brought us;
Facing the rising sun of our new day begun,
Let us march on till victory is won.

Stony the road we trod,
Bitter the chast'ning rod,
Felt in the days when hope unborn had died;
Yet with a steady beat,
Have not our weary feet
Come to the place for which our fathers sighed?
We have come over a way that with tears has been watered.
We have come, treading our path through the blood of the
    slaughtered,
Out from the gloomy past,
Till now we stand at last
Where the white gleam of our bright star is cast.

God of our weary years,
God of our silent tears,
Thou who hast brought us thus far on the way;
Thou who hast by Thy might,
Led us into the light,
Keep us forever in the path, we pray,
Lest our feet stray from the places, our God, where we met Thee,
Lest our hearts, drunk with the wine of the world, we forget Thee;
Shadowed beneath thy hand,
May we forever stand,
True to our God,
True to our native land.

PAUL LAURENCE DUNBAR
(1872–1906)

The son of ex-slaves, Dunbar was well established as a poet when he died of tuberculosis at the age of thirty-three. Though many of his poems are written in dialect, this, his best known work, is a clearly articulated and powerful cry from the heart belying the popular minstrel image of the laughing, dancing "darky."

We Wear the Mask

We wear the mask that grins and lies,
It hides our cheeks and shades our eyes—
This debt we pay to human guile;
With torn and bleeding hearts we smile,
And mouth with myriad subtleties.

Why should the world be over-wise,
In counting all our tears and sighs?
Nay, let them only see us, while
    We wear the mask.

We smile, but, O great Christ, our cries
To thee from tortured souls arise.
We sing, but oh the clay is vile
Beneath our feet, and long the mile;
But let the world dream otherwise,
    We wear the mask!

VACHEL LINDSAY
(1879–1931)

This is without doubt a racist poem, and was denounced as such by W. E. B. DuBois, among others, at the time of its publication in 1914. Lindsay himself would be considered a racist by our contemporary standards, in that he shared many of the racial attitudes of his time, but he defended himself to the NAACP as a promoter of African American contributions to society despite the handicaps of poverty and the heritage of slavery. He was also proud of his early sponsorship of the work of Langston Hughes (when Hughes was working as a busboy at a restaurant in Washington D.C. in 1910, he left copies of his poems at Lindsay's table when the poet was dining). What is undeniable is the rhetorical and musical power of this poem, which Lindsay performed in public many times, and which remains at its heart a tribute, however distorted, to the poetry and music of the black experience in America that is a fundamental part of our nation's culture.

The Congo
A Study of the Negro Race

I. THEIR BASIC SAVAGERY

Fat black bucks in a wine-barrel room,
Barrel-house kings, with feet unstable,

A deep rolling bass.

Sagged and reeled and pounded on the table,
Pounded on the table,
Beat an empty barrel with the handle of a broom,
Hard as they were able,
Boom, boom, Boom,
With a silk umbrella and the handle of a broom,
Boomlay, boomlay, boomlay, Boom.
Then I had religion, Then I had a vision.
I could not turn from their revel in derision.

More deliberate. Solemnly chanted.

Then I saw the Congo, creeping through the black,
Cutting through the forest with a golden track.
Then along that riverbank
A thousand miles
Tattooed cannibals danced in files;
Then I heard the boom of the blood-lust song

A rapidly piling climax of speed and racket.

And a thigh-bone beating on a tin-pan gong.
And "Blood" screamed the whistles and the fifes of the warriors,
"Blood" screamed the skull-faced, lean witch-doctors,
"Whirl ye the deadly voo-doo rattle,
Harry the uplands,
Steal all the cattle,
Rattle-rattle, rattle-rattle,
Bing.
Boomlay, boomlay, boomlay, Boom,"

With a philosophic pause.

A roaring, epic, rag-time tune
From the mouth of the Congo
To the Mountains of the Moon.
Death is an Elephant,

Shrilly and with a heavily accented metre.

Torch-eyed and horrible,
Foam-flanked and terrible.
Boom, steal the pygmies,
Boom, kill the Arabs,
Boom, kill the white men,
Hoo, Hoo, Hoo.

Like the wind in the chimney.

Listen to the yell of Leopold's ghost
Burning in Hell for his hand-maimed host.
Hear how the demons chuckle and yell
Cutting his hands off, down in Hell.
Listen to the creepy proclamation,
Blown through the lairs of the forest-nation,
Blown past the white-ants' hill of clay,
Blown past the marsh where the butterflies play:—
"Be careful what you do,

All the "o" sounds very golden. Heavy accents very heavy.
Light accents very light. Last line whispered.

Or Mumbo-Jumbo, God of the Congo,
And all of the other
Gods of the Congo,
Mumbo-Jumbo will hoo-doo you,
Mumbo-Jumbo will hoo-doo you,
Mumbo-Jumbo will hoo-doo you."

II. THEIR IRREPRESSIBLE HIGH SPIRITS

Rather shrill and high.

Wild crap-shooters with a whoop and a call
Danced the juba in their gambling hall
And laughed fit to kill, and shook the town,
And guyed the policemen and laughed them down
With a boomlay, boomlay, boomlay, Boom.

Read exactly as in first section.

Then I saw the Congo, creeping through the black,
Cutting through the forest with a golden track.

Lay emphasis on the delicate ideas.
Keep as light-footed as possible.

A negro fairyland swung into view,
A minstrel river
Where dreams come true.
The ebony palace soared on high
Through the blossoming trees to the evening sky.

The inlaid porches and casements shone
With gold and ivory and elephant-bone.
And the black crowd laughed till their sides were sore
At the baboon butler in the agate door,
And the well-known tunes of the parrot band
That trilled on the bushes of that magic land.

With pomposity.

A troupe of skull-faced witch-men came
Through the agate doorway in suits of flame,
Yea, long-tailed coats with a gold-leaf crust
And hats that were covered with diamond-dust.
And the crowd in the court gave a whoop and a call
And danced the juba from wall to wall.

With a great deliberation and ghostliness.

But the witch-men suddenly stilled the throng
With a stern cold glare, and a stern old song:—
"Mumbo-Jumbo will hoo-doo you." . . .

With overwhelming assurance, good cheer, and pomp.

Just then from the doorway, as fat as shoats,
Came the cake-walk princes in their long red coats,
Canes with a brilliant lacquer shine,
And tall silk hats that were red as wine.

With growing speed and sharply marked dance-rhythm.

And they pranced with their butterfly partners there,
Coal-black maidens with pearls in their hair,
Knee-skirts trimmed with the jassamine sweet,
And bells on their ankles and little black-feet.
And the couples railed at the chant and the frown
Of the witch-men lean, and laughed them down.
(Oh, rare was the revel, and well worth while
That made those glowering witch-men smile.)

The cake-walk royalty then began
To walk for a cake that was tall as a man
To the tune of "Boomlay, boomlay, Boom,"

With a touch of negro dialect,
and as rapidly as possible toward the end.

While the witch-men laughed, with a sinister air,
And sang with the scalawags prancing there:—
"Walk with care, walk with care,
Or Mumbo-Jumbo, God of the Congo,
And all of the other Gods of the Congo,
Mumbo-Jumbo will hoo-doo you.
Beware, beware, walk with care,
Boomlay, boomlay, boomlay, boom.
Boomlay, boomlay, boomlay, boom,
Boomlay, boomlay, boomlay, boom,
Boomlay, boomlay, boomlay,
Boom."

Slow philosophic calm.

(Oh, rare was the revel, and well worth while
That made those glowering witch-men smile.)

III. THE HOPE OF THEIR RELIGION

***Heavy bass. With a literal imitation
of camp-meeting racket, and trance.***

A good old negro in the slums of the town
Preached at a sister for her velvet gown.
Howled at a brother for his low-down ways,
His prowling, guzzling, sneak-thief days.
Beat on the Bible till he wore it out
Starting the jubilee revival shout.
And some had visions, as they stood on chairs,
And sang of Jacob, and the golden stairs,
And they all repented, a thousand strong
From their stupor and savagery and sin and wrong
And slammed with their hymn books till they shook the room
With "glory, glory, glory,"
And "Boom, boom, Boom."

***Exactly as in the first section.
Begin with terror and power, end with joy.***

Then I saw the Congo, creeping through the black,
Cutting through the jungle with a golden track.
And the gray sky opened like a new-rent veil
And showed the Apostles with their coats of mail.
In bright white steele they were seated round

And their fire-eyes watched where the Congo wound.
And the twelve Apostles, from their thrones on high
Thrilled all the forest with their heavenly cry:—

*Sung to the tune of "Hark, ten thousand
harps and voices."*

"Mumbo-Jumbo will die in the jungle;
Never again will he hoo-doo you,
Never again will he hoo-doo you."

With growing deliberation and joy.

Then along that river, a thousand miles
The vine-snared trees fell down in files.
Pioneer angels cleared the way
For a Congo paradise, for babes at play,
For sacred capitals, for temples clean.
Gone were the skull-faced witch-men lean.

In a rather high key—as delicately as possible.

There, where the wild ghost-gods had wailed
A million boats of the angels sailed
With oars of silver, and prows of blue
And silken pennants that the sun shone through.
'Twas a land transfigured, 'twas a new creation.
Oh, a singing wind swept the negro nation
And on through the backwoods clearing flew:—

To the tune of "Hark, ten thousand harps and voices."

"Mumbo-Jumbo is dead in the jungle.
Never again will he hoo-doo you.
Never again will he hoo-doo you."

Redeemed were the forests, the beasts and the men,
And only the vulture dared again
By the far, lone mountains of the moon
To cry, in the silence, the Congo tune:—

Dying down into a penetrating, terrified whisper.

"Mumbo-Jumbo will hoo-doo you,
Mumbo-Jumbo will hoo-doo you.
Mumbo . . . Jumbo . . . will . . . hoo-doo . . . you."

AMY LOWELL

(1874–1925)

Lowell, a member of the same Boston Brahmin family that included James Russell Lowell, became notorious for her openly lesbian lifestyle, which lent power and significance to her sometimes passionate poetry.

A Decade

When you came, you were like red wine and honey,
And the taste of you burnt my mouth with its sweetness.
Now you are like morning bread,
Smooth and pleasant.
I hardly taste you at all for I know your savor;
But I am completely nourished.

ROBERT FROST

(1874–1963)

Speaking at John F. Kennedy's inauguration in 1961, where he recited "The Gift Outright" from memory when unable to read the pages he had written especially for the occasion, Frost seemed the very essence of American poetry, a craggy repository of traditional values. This image, and the fact that he wrote using familiar metrics and rhyme schemes, damaged his critical reputation in the years immediately following his death. But any careful reading of Frost's poetry reveals a sharp and sometimes coldly analytic view of human nature to rival any of the later American poets generally seen as more modern than he.

Reversing the reader's initial expectations of this poem, Frost gradually makes it clear that the gift of the title was not the land of America to its settlers, but the gift of the lifeblood of our forebears as they transformed the continent into our own nation.

The Gift Outright

The land was ours before we were the land's.
She was our land more than a hundred years
Before we were her people. She was ours
In Massachusetts, in Virginia,
But we were England's, still colonials,
Possessing what we still were unpossessed by,
Possessed by what we now no more possessed.
Something we were withholding made us weak
Until we found out that it was ourselves

We were withholding from our land of living,
And forthwith found salvation in surrender.
Such as we were we gave ourselves outright
(The deed of gift was many deeds of war)
To the land vaguely realizing westward,
But still unstoried, artless, unenhanced,
Such as she was, such as she would become.

The theme of this poem is not as obvious as it may seem at first. Taking the road less traveled appeals to the traditional American spirit of individuality, but it's notable that the poet expects to spend his life recalling his choice with a sigh.

The Road Not Taken

Two roads diverged in a yellow wood,
And sorry I could not travel both
And be one traveler, long I stood
And looked down one as far as I could
To where it bent in the undergrowth;

Then took the other, as just as fair,
And having perhaps the better claim,
Because it was grassy and wanted wear;
Though as for that the passing there
Had worn them really about the same,

And both that morning equally lay
In leaves no step had trodden black.
Oh, I kept the first for another day!
Yet knowing how way leads on to way,
I doubted if I should ever come back.

I shall be telling this with a sigh
Somewhere ages and ages hence:
Two roads diverged in a wood, and I—
I took the one less traveled by,
And that has made all the difference.

The very structure of this poem seems to lend it authority as well as beauty, especially the repetition of rhyme and words in the last four lines. As with a number of Frost's greatest poems, the simple rustic beauty of the scene described here becomes transformed into a meditation on life and death.

Stopping by Woods on a Snowy Evening

Whose woods these are I think I know.
His house is in the village though;
He will not see me stopping here
To watch his woods fill up with snow.

My little horse must think it's queer
To stop without a farmhouse near
Between the woods and frozen lake
The darkest evening of the year.

He gives his harness bells a shake
To ask if there's some mistake.
The only other sound's the sweep
Of easy wind and downy flake.

The woods are lovely, dark, and deep,
But I have promises to keep,
And miles to go before I sleep,
And miles to go before I sleep.

In this masterful vignette, Frost seems at first to be recounting a seasonal rustic chore—two neighbors fixing a wall after a hard winter. But while one neighbor—the poet—lightly ridicules the significance of such an antiquated means of marking property, the other simply repeats his mantra—"Good fences make good neighbors"—as he moves in darkness, a stone in each hand, like weapons.

Mending Wall

Something there is that doesn't love a wall,
That sends the frozen-ground-swell under it,
And spills the upper boulders in the sun,
And makes gaps even two can pass abreast.
The work of hunters is another thing:
I have come after them and made repair
Where they have left not one stone on a stone,
But they would have the rabbit out of hiding,
To please the yelping dogs. The gaps I mean,
No one has seen them made or heard them made,
But at spring mending-time we find them there.
I let my neighbor know beyond the hill;
And on a day we meet to walk the line
And set the wall between us once again.
We keep the wall between us as we go.
To each the boulders that have fallen to each.
And some are loaves and some so nearly balls
We have to use a spell to make them balance:
'Stay where you are until our backs are turned!'
We wear our fingers rough with handling them.

Oh, just another kind of outdoor game,
One on a side. It comes to little more:
There where it is we do not need the wall:
He is all pine and I am apple orchard.
My apple trees will never get across
And eat the cones under his pines, I tell him.
He only says, 'Good fences make good neighbors.'
Spring is the mischief in me, and I wonder
If I could put a notion in his head:
'Why do they make good neighbors? Isn't it
Where there are cows? But here there are no cows.
Before I built a wall I'd ask to know
What I was walling in or walling out,
And to whom I was like to give offence.
Something there is that doesn't love a wall,
That wants it down.' I could say 'Elves' to him,
But it's not elves exactly, and I'd rather
He said it for himself. I see him there
Bringing a stone grasped firmly by the top
In each hand, like an old-stone savage armed.
He moves in darkness as it seems to me,
Not of woods only and the shade of trees.
He will not go behind his father's saying,
And he likes having thought of it so well
He says again, 'Good fences make good neighbors.'

Silas the hired hand has outlived his usefulness; his only skill is stacking hay. He has come home to die, but where is his true home? Frost's answer continues to resonate in our modern, transient culture.

Unlike most of his poems, this one is written largely in blank verse, but in a powerful dialogue that carries the poem along. Frost famously deprecated the idea of writing in free verse, comparing it to playing tennis with the net down!

Death of the Hired Man

Mary sat musing on the lamp-flame at the table
Waiting for Warren. When she heard his step,
She ran on tip-toe down the darkened passage
To meet him in the doorway with the news
And put him on his guard. "Silas is back."
She pushed him outward with her through the door
And shut it after her. "Be kind," she said.
She took the market things from Warren's arms
And set them on the porch, then drew him down
To sit beside her on the wooden steps.

"When was I ever anything but kind to him?
But I'll not have the fellow back," he said.
"I told him so last haying, didn't I?
If he left then, I said, that ended it.
What good is he? Who else will harbor him
At his age for the little he can do?
What help he is there's no depending on.
Off he goes always when I need him most.

He thinks he ought to earn a little pay,
Enough at least to buy tobacco with,
So he won't have to beg and be beholden.
'All right,' I say, 'I can't afford to pay
Any fixed wages, though I wish I could.'
'Someone else can.' 'Then someone else will have to.'
I shouldn't mind his bettering himself
If that was what it was. You can be certain,
When he begins like that, there's someone at him
Trying to coax him off with pocket-money,—
In haying time, when any help is scarce.
In winter he comes back to us. I'm done."

"Sh! not so loud: he'll hear you," Mary said.

"I want him to: he'll have to soon or late."

"He's worn out. He's asleep beside the stove.
When I came up from Rowe's I found him here,
Huddled against the barn-door fast asleep,
A miserable sight, and frightening, too—
You needn't smile—I didn't recognize him—
I wasn't looking for him—and he's changed.
Wait till you see."

                "Where did you say he'd been?"

"He didn't say. I dragged him to the house,
And gave him tea and tried to make him smoke.
I tried to make him talk about his travels.
Nothing would do: he just kept nodding off."

"What did he say? Did he say anything?"

"But little."

        "Anything? Mary, confess
He said he'd come to ditch the meadow for me."

"Warren!"

        "But did he? I just want to know."

"Of course he did. What would you have him say?
Surely you wouldn't grudge the poor old man
Some humble way to save his self-respect.
He added, if you really care to know,
He meant to clear the upper pasture, too.
That sounds like something you have heard before?
Warren, I wish you could have heard the way
He jumbled everything. I stopped to look
Two or three times—he made me feel so queer—
To see if he was talking in his sleep.
He ran on Harold Wilson—you remember—
The boy you had in haying four years since.
He's finished school, and teaching in his college.
Silas declares you'll have to get him back.
He says they two will make a team for work:
Between them they will lay this farm as smooth!
The way he mixed that in with other things.
He thinks young Wilson a likely lad, though daft
On education—you know how they fought
All through July under the blazing sun,
Silas up on the cart to build the load,
Harold along beside to pitch it on."

"Yes, I took care to keep well out of earshot."

"Well, those days trouble Silas like a dream.
You wouldn't think they would. How some things linger!
Harold's young college boy's assurance piqued him.
After so many years he still keeps finding
Good arguments he sees he might have used.
I sympathize. I know just how it feels
To think of the right thing to say too late.
Harold's associated in his mind with Latin.
He asked me what I thought of Harold's saying
He studied Latin like the violin
Because he liked it—that an argument!
He said he couldn't make the boy believe
He could find water with a hazel prong—
Which showed how much good school had ever done him.
He wanted to go over that. But most of all
He thinks if he could have another chance
To teach him how to build a load of hay—"

"I know, that's Silas' one accomplishment.
He bundles every forkful in its place,
And tags and numbers it for future reference,
So he can find and easily dislodge it
In the unloading. Silas does that well.
He takes it out in bunches like big birds' nests.
You never see him standing on the hay
He's trying to lift, straining to lift himself."

"He thinks if he could teach him that, he'd be
Some good perhaps to someone in the world.
He hates to see a boy the fool of books.
Poor Silas, so concerned for other folk,
And nothing to look backward to with pride,
And nothing to look forward to with hope,
So now and never any different."

Part of a moon was falling down the west,
Dragging the whole sky with it to the hills.
Its light poured softly in her lap. She saw it
And spread her apron to it. She put out her hand
Among the harp-like morning-glory strings,
Taut with the dew from garden bed to eaves,
As if she played unheard the tenderness
That wrought on him beside her in the night.
"Warren," she said, "he has come home to die:
You needn't be afraid he'll leave you this time."

"Home," he mocked gently.

                        "Yes, what else but home?
It all depends on what you mean by home.
Of course he's nothing to us, any more
Than was the hound that came a stranger to us
Out of the woods, worn out upon the trail."

"Home is the place where, when you have to go there,
They have to take you in."

                        "I should have called it
Something you somehow haven't to deserve."

Warren leaned out and took a step or two,
Picked up a little stick, and brought it back
And broke it in his hand and tossed it by.
"Silas has better claim on us you think
Than on his brother? Thirteen little miles
As the road winds would bring him to his door.
Silas has walked that far no doubt today.
Why doesn't he go there? His brother's rich,
A somebody—director in the bank."

"He never told us that."

                                   "We know it though."
"I think his brother ought to help, of course.
I'll see to that if there is need. He ought of right
To take him in, and might be willing to—
He may be better than appearances.
But have some pity on Silas. Do you think
If he'd had any pride in claiming kin
Or anything he looked for from his brother,
He'd keep so still about him all this time?"

"I wonder what's between them."

                                      "I can tell you.
Silas is what he is—we wouldn't mind him—
But just the kind that kinsfolk can't abide.
He never did a thing so very bad.
He don't know why he isn't quite as good
As anybody. Worthless though he is,
He won't be made ashamed
to please his brother."

"*I* can't think Si ever hurt anyone."

"No, but he hurt my heart the way he lay
And rolled his old head on that sharp-edged chair-back.
He wouldn't let me put him on the lounge.
You must go in and see what you can do.
I made the bed up for him there tonight.
You'll be surprised at him—how much he's broken.
His working days are done; I'm sure of it."

"I'd not be in a hurry to say that."

"I haven't been. Go, look, see for yourself.
But, Warren, please remember how it is:
He's come to help you ditch the meadow.
He has a plan. You mustn't laugh at him.
He may not speak of it, and then he may.
I'll sit and see if that small sailing cloud
Will hit or miss the moon."

It hit the moon.
Then there were three there, making a dim row,
The moon, the little silver cloud, and she.

Warren returned—too soon, it seemed to her,
Slipped to her side, caught up her hand and waited.

"Warren," she questioned.

"Dead," was all he answered.

CARL SANDBURG

(1878–1967)

Carl Sandburg was born poor in Galesburg, Illinois, and after an adventurous youth (including serving in the U.S. Army in Cuba during the Spanish-American War), he settled in Chicago with his wife, the sister of the photographer Edward Steichen. At times a fervent socialist and always a populist, Sandburg wrote of America in a free verse that was sometimes reminiscent of Whitman, but with a postindustrial note. Often he strove for a single unifying moment in his poems, with an almost haiku-like effect.

"Chicago" is perhaps Sandburg's most Whitman-like poem, but it is more about things than the people or ideas Whitman usually chose as his subjects. Whitman created great art, while Sandburg can be considered more a brilliant illustrator of memorable images.

Chicago

Hog Butcher for the World,
Tool Maker, Stacker of Wheat,
Player with Railroads and the Nation's Freight Handler;
Stormy, husky, brawling,
City of the Big Shoulders:

They tell me you are wicked and I believe them, for I have seen your
   painted women under the gas lamps luring the farm boys.
And they tell me you are crooked and I answer: Yes, it is true I have
   seen the gunman kill and go free to kill again.
And they tell me you are brutal and my reply is: On the faces of
   women and children I have seen the marks of wanton hunger.
And having answered so I turn once more to those who sneer at this
   my city, and I give them back the sneer and say to them:
Come and show me another city with lifted head singing so proud to
   be alive and coarse and strong and cunning.
Flinging magnetic curses amid the toil of piling job on job, here is a
   tall bold slugger set vivid against the little soft cities;
Fierce as a dog with tongue lapping for action, cunning as a savage
   pitted against the wilderness,
      Bareheaded,
      Shoveling,
      Wrecking,
      Planning,
      Building, breaking, rebuilding,
Under the smoke, dust all over his mouth, laughing with white
   teeth,
Under the terrible burden of destiny laughing as a young man
   laughs,
Laughing even as an ignorant fighter laughs who has never lost a
   battle,
Bragging and laughing that under his wrist is the pulse, and under
   his ribs the heart of the people,
         Laughing!
Laughing the stormy, husky, brawling laughter of Youth, half-naked,
   sweating, proud to be Hog Butcher, Tool Maker, Stacker of
   Wheat, Player with Railroads and Freight Handler to the Nation.

This poem creates only a single metaphor, but an unforgettable one.

Fog

The fog comes
on little cat feet.

It sits looking
over harbor and city
on silent haunches
and then moves on.

This poem shows Sandburg's social concerns, yet again with a powerful central image that makes the poem more than a simple antiwar homily.

Grass

Pile the bodies high at Austerlitz and Waterloo.
Shovel them under and let me work—
　　　　I am the grass; I cover all.

And pile them high at Gettysburg
And pile them high at Ypres and Verdun.
Shovel them under and let me work.
Two years, ten years, and the passengers ask the conductor:
　　　　What place is this?
　　　　Where are we now?

　　　　I am the grass.
　　　　Let me work.

WALLACE STEVENS

(1879–1955)

Wallace Stevens lived a double life—a prominent insurance executive in Hartford, Connecticut, he was also one of the most imaginative and daringly creative American poets of the twentieth century. Writing at a time when Freud was promulgating the idea of the role of the unconscious mind in everyday life, Stevens showed how the imagination can create beauty and significance from expressive imagery that defies logical analysis.

This sensuous poem, filled with alliteration and internal rhyme, is an acknowledgment of the enduring vitality of daily life in the face of death.

The Emperor of Ice-Cream

Call the roller of big cigars,
The muscular one, and bid him whip
In kitchen cups concupiscent curds.
Let the wenches dawdle in such dress
As they are used to wear, and let the boys
Bring flowers in last month's newspapers.
Let be be finale of seem.
The only emperor is the emperor of ice-cream.

Take from the dresser of deal,
Lacking the three glass knobs, that sheet
On which she embroidered fantails once
And spread it so as to cover her face.
If her horny feet protrude, they come
To show how cold she is, and dumb.
Let the lamp affix its beam.
The only emperor is the emperor of ice-cream.

This poem offers extraordinarily diverse variations on a theme, or rather an image that can be transformed almost endlessly. The early verses evoke Japanese haiku; some of the later ones seem almost like glosses of a Robert Frost poem.

Thirteen Ways of Looking at a Blackbird

1

Among twenty snowy mountains,
The only moving thing
Was the eye of the blackbird.

2

I was of three minds,
Like a tree
In which there are three blackbirds.

3

The blackbird whirled in the autumn winds.
It was a small part of the pantomime.

4

A man and a woman
Are one.
A man and a woman and a blackbird
Are one.

5

I do not know which to prefer,
The beauty of inflections
Or the beauty of innuendoes,
The blackbird whistling
Or just after.

6

Icicles filled the long window
With barbaric glass.
The shadow of the blackbird
Crossed it to and fro.
The mood
Traced in the shadow
An indecipherable cause.

7

O thin men of Haddam,
Why do you imagine golden birds?
Do you not see how the blackbird
Walks around the feet
Of the women about you?

8

I know noble accents
And lucid, inescapable rhythms;
But I know, too,
That the blackbird is involved
In what I know.

9

When the blackbird flew out of sight,
It marked the edge
Of one of many circles.

10

At the sight of blackbirds
Flying in a green light,
Even the bawds of euphony
Would cry out sharply.

11

He rode over Connecticut
In a glass coach.
Once, a fear pierced him
In that he mistook
The shadow of his equipage
For blackbirds.

12

The river is moving.
The blackbird must be flying.

13

It was evening all afternoon.
It was snowing
And it was going to snow.
The blackbird sat
In the cedar-limbs.

EDGAR GUEST

(1881–1959)

This poem is extremely sentimental and could even be described as banal, with its cornball dialect and down-home attitudes, but it is in a strong American tradition of honoring what are assumed to be traditional values. Guest was an enormously popular versifier who for many years wrote a daily poem for hundreds of newspapers across the country.

Home

It takes a heap o' livin' in a house t' make it home,
A heap o' sun an' shadder, an' ye sometimes have t' roam
Afore ye really 'preciate the things ye lef' behind,
An' hunger fer 'em somehow, with 'em allus on yer mind.
It don't make any differunce how rich ye get t' be,
How much yer chairs an' tables cost, how great yer luxury;
It ain't home t' ye, though it be the palace of a king,
Until somehow yer soul is sort o' wrapped round everything.

Home ain't a place that gold can buy or get up in a minute;
Afore it's home there's got t' be a heap o' livin' in it;
Within the walls there's got t' be some babies born, and then
Right there ye've got t' bring 'em up t' women good, an' men;
And gradjerly as time goes on, ye find ye wouldn't part
With anything they ever used—they've grown into yer heart:
The old high chairs, the playthings, too, the little shoes they wore
Ye hoard; an' if ye could ye'd keep the thumb marks on the door.

Ye've got t' weep t' make it home, ye've got t' sit an' sigh
An' watch beside a loved one's bed, an' know that Death is nigh;
An' in the stillness o' the night t' see Death's angel come,
An' close the eyes o' her that smiled, an' leave her sweet voice dumb.
Fer these are scenes that grip the heart, an' when yer tears are dried,
Ye find the home is dearer than it was, an' sanctified;
An' tuggin' at ye always are the pleasant memories
O' her that was an' is no more—ye can't escape from these.

Ye've got t' sing an' dance fer years, ye've got t' romp an' play,
An' learn t' love the things ye have by usin' 'em each day;
Even the roses 'round the porch must blossom year by year
Afore they 'come a part o' ye, suggestin' someone dear
Who used t' love 'em long ago, an' trained 'em jes t' run
The way they do, so's they would get the early mornin' sun;
Ye've got t' love each brick an' stone from cellar up t' dome:
It takes a heap o' livin' in a house t' make it home.

WILLIAM CARLOS WILLIAMS
(1883–1963)

During the many years Williams spent as a pediatrician in Paterson, New Jersey, he actively promoted the development of modern poetry in America, influenced by his early acquaintance with Ezra Pound, among others. Like Wallace Stevens, Williams communicated largely through powerful imagery, though usually within a simple yet elegant verse structure.

This poem seems almost like an extended caption for a rustic still life painting, but a sense of urgency belies the tranquil imagery.

The Red Wheelbarrow

so much depends
upon

a red wheel
barrow

glazed with rain
water

beside the white
chickens.

Written as though it were a message attached to a refrigerator door, this poem is simultaneously innocent and sensual. Its effect is heightened by the normality of its setting and the deceptive simplicity of its language.

This Is Just to Say

I have eaten
the plums
that were in
the icebox

and which
you were probably
saving
for breakfast

Forgive me
they were delicious
so sweet
and so cold

EZRA POUND

(1885–1972)

Ezra Pound is celebrated as a powerful influence on modern poetry, though his legacy has been darkened by his virulent anti-Semitism and adherence to the cause of Mussolini during the Second World War, when he lived in Italy and broadcast Fascist propaganda. Much of his poetry is esoteric and obscure, but the work below, a parody of a traditional English lyric, shows Pound to have had a characteristically wry American sense of humor.

Ancient Music

Note.—This is not folk music, but Dr. Ker writes that the tune is to be found under the Latin words of a very ancient canon. [Pound's note]

Winter is icummen in,
Lhude sing Goddamm.
Raineth drop and staineth slop,
And how the wind doth ramm!
   Sing: Goddamm.
Skiddeth bus and sloppeth us,
An ague hath my ham.
Freezeth river, turneth liver,
   Damn you, sing: Goddamm.
Goddamm, Goddamm, 'tis why I am, Goddamm,
   So 'gainst the winter's balm.
Sing goddamm, damm, sing Goddamm.
Sing goddamm, sing goddamm, DAMM.

JOYCE KILMER
(1886–1918)

Kilmer died in Europe, a casualty of the Great War. His most famous poem is a tangled mixture of ill-assorted metaphors, but with its reverent, nature-loving sentiments it has become embedded in our popular culture.

Trees

I think that I shall never see
A poem lovely as a tree.

A tree whose hungry mouth is prest
Against the sweet earth's flowing breast;

A tree that looks at God all day,
And lifts her leafy arms to pray;

A tree that may in summer wear
A nest of robins in her hair;

Upon whose bosom snow has lain;
Who intimately lives with rain.

Poems are made by fools like me,
But only God can make a tree.

MARIANNE MOORE

(1887–1972)

Marianne Moore lived with her mother most of her life, and never married. She was an early admirer and acquaintance of such modern poets as Ezra Pound, Wallace Stevens, and William Carlos Williams (who said of her work that "in looking at some apparently small object, one feels the swirl of great events"). Like Stevens and Williams, Moore undeniably sought out powerful images that communicate directly from poet to reader without the necessity of logical thought. At the same time, she was fascinated by natural phenomena, and wrote some of her most notable poems about animals. She was famously a baseball fan, and rooted for—and wrote poems about—the Brooklyn Dodgers. Becoming something of a legendary and eccentric figure in her old age, she was asked by the Ford Motor Company to help them name a new car; they rejected all her suggestions and named it the Edsel!

For all her love of the imagery and allusiveness of modern poetry, Moore was keenly aware of the need for the poet to stay anchored in the real world, which occasioned her most famous poem, below. It was first published in 1919, in the midst of the poetic revolution represented by the modernist school led by Pound.

Poetry

I, too, dislike it: there are things that are important beyond all this
    fiddle.
  Reading it, however, with a perfect contempt for it, one discovers in
  it after all, a place for the genuine.
    Hands that can grasp, eyes
    that can dilate, hair that can rise
      if it must, these things are important not because a

high-sounding interpretation can be put upon them but because
    they are
  useful. When they become so derivative as to become
    unintelligible,
  the same thing may be said for all of us, that we
    do not admire what
    we cannot understand: the bat
      holding on upside down or in quest of something to

eat, elephants pushing, a wild horse taking a roll, a tireless wolf under
a tree, the immovable critic twitching his skin like a horse that
feels a flea, the base-
ball fan, the statistician—
nor is it valid
to discriminate against 'business documents and

school-books'; all these phenomena are important. One must make a
distinction
however: when dragged into prominence by half poets, the result
is not poetry,
nor till the poets among us can be
'literalists of
the imagination'—above
insolence and triviality and can present

for inspection, 'imaginary gardens with real toads in them', shall we
have it. In the meantime, if you demand on the one hand,
the raw material of poetry in
all its rawness and
that which is on the other hand
genuine, you are interested in poetry.

THOMAS STEARNS ELIOT

(1888–1965)

Eliot was one of the emblematic poets of the twentieth century. He was greatly influenced by Ezra Pound, but because Eliot's poetry has greater power and accessibility than Pound's, he has had a more lasting impact on the reading public. Eliot was a contemporary of modern poets like Stevens and Williams (who criticized his work as being too academic), but unlike those poets, whose creative work was done while they were occupied in careers in insurance and medicine, Eliot was a professional writer of poetry, critical essays, and drama; his only other significant occupation was as an editor, both of literary magazines and for some time with the British publishing house of Faber and Faber (where he notably rejected George Orwell's submission of *Animal Farm*). During his lifetime Eliot was lauded for his erudition and for the tone of disillusionment and despair that pervaded his work, and seemed to some the characteristic theme of his times. Since his death his later work has become less celebrated (except for the atypically playful *Old Possum's Book of Practical Cats,* the source of the enormously successful Broadway musical *Cats*), and his personal reputation has been darkened by his anti-Semitism (which he shared with Pound and others of their circle) and the ambiguous deterioration of his marriage (he had his wife of many years committed to a sanitarium for the mentally ill).

Nonetheless, his early work remains a powerful statement of a personal crisis of faith written with an essential poetic eloquence and psychological insight that has survived the vicissitudes of its author's reputation.

The epigraph of this poem, from Dante's *Inferno*, indicates the speaker's willingness to admit his crimes only in the belief (clearly and ironically misguided) that his confession would never be made known to the world. Similarly, in the poem Prufrock confesses his sense of inadequacy almost as though he were a patient speaking to his psychoanalyst, but the echoes of his fears resound down the years, as though he were speaking for all of us.

The Love Song of J. Alfred Prufrock

S'io credesse che mia risposta fosse
A persona che mai tornasse al mondo,
Questa fiamma staria senza piu scosse.
Ma perciocche giammai di questo fondo
Non torno vivo alcun, s'i'odo il vero,
Senza tema d'infamia ti rispondo.

Let us go then, you and I,
When the evening is spread out against the sky
Like a patient etherized upon a table;
Let us go, through certain half-deserted streets,
The muttering retreats
Of restless nights in one-night cheap hotels
And sawdust restaurants with oyster-shells:
Streets that follow like a tedious argument
Of insidious intent
To lead you to an overwhelming question . . .
Oh, do not ask, "What is it?"
Let us go and make our visit.

In the room the women come and go
Talking of Michelangelo.

   The yellow fog that rubs its back upon the window-panes,
The yellow smoke that rubs its muzzle on the window-panes
Licked its tongue into the corners of the evening,
Lingered upon the pools that stand in drains,
Let fall upon its back the soot that falls from chimneys,
Slipped by the terrace, made a sudden leap,
And seeing that it was a soft October night,
Curled once about the house, and fell asleep.

   And indeed there will be time
For the yellow smoke that slides along the street,
Rubbing its back upon the window-panes;
There will be time, there will be time
To prepare a face to meet the faces that you meet;
There will be time to murder and create,
And time for all the works and days of hands
That lift and drop a question on your plate;
Time for you and time for me,
And time yet for a hundred indecisions,
And for a hundred visions and revisions,
Before the taking of a toast and tea.

   In the room the women come and go
Talking of Michelangelo.

And indeed there will be time
To wonder, "Do I dare?" and, "Do I dare?"
Time to turn back and descend the stair,
With a bald spot in the middle of my hair—
[They will say: "How his hair is growing thin!"]

My morning coat, my collar mounting firmly to the chin,
My necktie rich and modest, but asserted by a simple pin—
[They will say: "But how his arms and legs are thin!"]
Do I dare
Disturb the universe?
In a minute there is time
For decisions and revisions which a minute will reverse.

   For I have known them all already, known them all—
Have known the evenings, mornings, afternoons,
I have measured out my life with coffee spoons;
I know the voices dying with a dying fall
Beneath the music from a farther room.
   So how should I presume?

   And I have known the eyes already, known them all—
The eyes that fix you in a formulated phrase,
And when I am formulated, sprawling on a pin,
When I am pinned and wriggling on the wall,
Then how should I begin
To spit out all the butt-ends of my days and ways?
   And how should I presume?

   And I have known the arms already, known them all—
Arms that are braceleted and white and bare
[But in the lamplight, downed with light brown hair!]
Is it perfume from a dress
That makes me so digress?
Arms that lie along a table, or wrap about a shawl.
   And should I then presume?
   And how should I begin?

      . . . . .

Shall I say, I have gone at dusk through narrow streets
And watched the smoke that rises from the pipes
Of lonely men in shirt-sleeves, leaning out of windows? . . .

I should have been a pair of ragged claws
Scuttling across the floors of silent seas.

. . . . .

And the afternoon, the evening, sleeps so peacefully!
Smoothed by long fingers,
Asleep . . . tired . . . or it malingers,
Stretched on the floor, here beside you and me.
Should I, after tea and cakes and ices,
Have the strength to force the moment to its crisis?
But though I have wept and fasted, wept and prayed,
Though I have seen my head [grown slightly bald] brought in upon
a platter,
I am no prophet—and here's no great matter;
I have seen the moment of my greatness flicker,
And I have seen the eternal Footman hold my coat, and snicker,
And in short, I was afraid.

And would it have been worth it, after all,
After the cups, the marmalade, the tea,
Among the porcelain, among some talk of you and me,
Would it have been worth while,
To have bitten off the matter with a smile,
To have squeezed the universe into a ball
To roll it toward some overwhelming question,
To say: "I am Lazarus, come from the dead,
Come back to tell you all, I shall tell you all"—
If one, settling a pillow by her head,
Should say: "That is not what I meant at all.
That is not it, at all."

And would it have been worth it, after all,
Would it have been worth while,
After the sunsets and the dooryards and the sprinkled streets,
After the novels, after the teacups, after the skirts that trail along the
    floor—
And this, and so much more?—
It is impossible to say just what I mean!
But as if a magic lantern threw the nerves in patterns on a screen:
Would it have been worth while
If one, settling a pillow or throwing off a shawl,
And turning toward the window, should say:
   "That is not it at all,
   That is not what I meant, at all."

     . . . . .

No I am not Prince Hamlet, nor was meant to be;
Am an attendant lord, one that will do
To swell a progress, start a scene or two,
Advise the prince; no doubt, an easy tool,
Deferential, glad to be of use,
Politic, cautious, and meticulous;
Full of high sentence, but a bit obtuse;
At times, indeed, almost ridiculous—
Almost, at times, the Fool.

   I grow old . . . I grow old . . .
I shall wear the bottoms of my trousers rolled.

   Shall I part my hair behind? Do I dare to eat a peach?
I shall wear white flannel trousers, and walk upon the beach.
I have heard the mermaids singing, each to each.

   I do not think that they will sing to me.

I have seen them riding seaward on the waves
Combing the white hair of the waves blown back
When the wind blows the water white and black.

We have lingered in the chambers of the sea
By sea-girls wreathed with seaweed red and brown
Till human voices wake us, and we drown.

The personal alienation Eliot expressed in "The Love Song of J. Alfred Prufrock" escalated to a monumental level of dread and disgust in *The Waste Land* (the poem's epigraph recounts a question put to the Cumaean Sybil: "What do you want?" and the answer: "I want to die."). At the same time, the power, erudition, and technical mastery displayed in this work gained for its author unparalleled recognition as a poet, demoralizing his modernist peers. William Carlos Williams recalled the publication of *The Waste Land* this way:

> Then out of the blue *The Dial* brought out *The Waste Land* and all our hilarity ended. It wiped out our world as if an atom bomb had been dropped upon it and our brave sallies into the unknown were turned to dust.

But the poem's very knottiness and inaccessibility (even the appended clarifying notes, added at the request of his publisher so that the poem could be brought out in a book-length version, do more to emphasize the author's knowledge and authority than to explain the text) left a baleful influence on those who were to follow Eliot. In some sense the appearance of *The Waste Land,* often acclaimed as the greatest poem in English of the twentieth century, fostered an atmosphere of esoteric elitism that poets like Williams spent years trying to overcome.

The Waste Land
1922

*"Nam Sibyllam quidem Cumis ego ipse oculis meis vidi in ampulla
pendere, et cum illi pueri dicerent:* Σίβυλλα τί θέλεις; *(respondebat illa:*
ἀποθανεῖν θέλω.*"*

For Ezra Pound

il miglior fabbro.

I. THE BURIAL OF THE DEAD

April is the cruellest month, breeding
Lilacs out of the dead land, mixing
Memory and desire, stirring
Dull roots with spring rain.
Winter kept us warm, covering
Earth in forgetful snow, feeding
A little life with dried tubers.
Summer surprised us, coming over the Starnbergersee
With a shower of rain; we stopped in the colonnade,
And went on in sunlight, into the Hofgarten,
And drank coffee, and talked for an hour.
Bin gar keine Russin, stamm' aus Litauen, echt deutsch.
And when we were children, staying at the archduke's,
My cousin's, he took me out on a sled,
And I was frightened. He said, Marie,
Marie, hold on tight. And down we went.
In the mountains, there you feel free.
I read, much of the night, and go south in the winter.

What are the roots that clutch, what branches grow
Out of this stony rubbish? Son of man,
You cannot say, or guess, for you know only
A heap of broken images, where the sun beats,
And the dead tree gives no shelter, the cricket no relief,
And the dry stone no sound of water. Only
There is shadow under this red rock,
(Come in under the shadow of this red rock),
And I will show you something different from either
Your shadow at morning striding behind you
Or your shadow at evening rising to meet you;
I will show you fear in a handful of dust.

> *Frisch weht der Wind*
> *Der Heimat zu*
> *Mein Irisch Kind,*
> *Wo weilest du?*

"You gave me hyacinths first a year ago;
"They called me the hyacinth girl."
—Yet when we came back, late, from the Hyacinth garden,
Your arms full, and your hair wet, I could not
Speak, and my eyes failed, I was neither
Living nor dead, and I knew nothing,
Looking into the heart of light, the silence.
Oed' und leer das Meer.

Madame Sosostris, famous clairvoyante,
Had a bad cold, nevertheless
Is known to be the wisest woman in Europe,
With a wicked pack of cards. Here, said she,
Is your card, the drowned Phoenician Sailor,
(Those are pearls that were his eyes. Look!)
Here is Belladonna, the Lady of the Rocks,
The lady of situations.

Here is the man with three staves, and here the Wheel,
And here is the one-eyed merchant, and this card,
Which is blank, is something he carries on his back,
Which I am forbidden to see. I do not find
The Hanged Man. Fear death by water.
I see crowds of people, walking round in a ring.
Thank you. If you see dear Mrs. Equitone,
Tell her I bring the horoscope myself:
One must be so careful these days.

    Unreal City,
Under the brown fog of a winter dawn,
A crowd flowed over London Bridge, so many,
I had not thought death had undone so many.
Sighs, short and infrequent, were exhaled,
And each man fixed his eyes before his feet.
Flowed up the hill and down King William Street,
To where Saint Mary Woolnoth kept the hours
With a dead sound on the final stroke of nine.
There I saw one I knew, and stopped him, crying: "Stetson!
"You who were with me in the ships at Mylae!
"That corpse you planted last year in your garden,
"Has it begun to sprout? Will it bloom this year?
"Or has the sudden frost disturbed its bed?
"Oh keep the Dog far hence, that's friend to men,
"Or with his nails he'll dig it up again!
"You! hypocrite lecteur!—mon semblable,—mon frère!"

II. A GAME OF CHESS

The Chair she sat in, like a burnished throne,
Glowed on the marble, where the glass
Held up by standards wrought with fruited vines

From which a golden Cupidon peeped out
(Another hid his eyes behind his wing)
Doubled the flames of sevenbranched candelabra
Reflecting light upon the table as
The glitter of her jewels rose to meet it.
From satin cases poured in rich profusion;
In vials of ivory and coloured glass
Unstoppered, lurked her strange synthetic perfumes,
Unguent, powdered, or liquid—troubled, confused
And drowned the sense in odours; stirred by the air
That freshened from the window, these ascended
In fattening the prolonged candle-flames,
Flung their smoke into the laquearia,
Stirring the pattern on the coffered ceiling.
Huge sea-wood fed with copper
Burned green and orange, framed by the coloured stone,
In which sad light a carvèd dolphin swam.
Above the antique mantel was displayed
As though a window gave upon the sylvan scene
The change of Philomel, by the barbarous king
So rudely forced; yet there the nightingale
Filled all the desert with inviolable voice
And still she cried, and still the world pursues,
"Jug Jug" to dirty ears.
And other withered stumps of time
Were told upon the walls; staring forms
Leaned out, leaning, hushing the room enclosed.
Footsteps shuffled on the stair.
Under the firelight, under the brush, her hair
Spread out in fiery points
Glowed into words, then would be savagely still.

"My nerves are bad to-night. Yes, bad. Stay with me.
"Speak to me. Why do you never speak. Speak.
　　"What are you thinking of? What thinking? What?
"I never know what you are thinking. Think."

　　I think we are in rats' alley
Where the dead men lost their bones.

　　"What is that noise?"
　　　　　　　　　　　The wind under the door.
"What is that noise now? What is the wind doing?"
　　　　　　　　　　Nothing again nothing.
　　　　　　　　　　　　　　　　"Do
"You know nothing? Do you see nothing? Do you remember
"Nothing?"

　　　　I remember
Those are pearls that were his eyes.
"Are you alive, or not? Is there nothing in your head?"
　　　　　　　　　　　　　　　　　　But

O O O O that Shakespeherian Rag—
It's so elegant
So intelligent
"What shall I do now? What shall I do?"
"I shall rush out as I am, and walk the street
"With my hair down, so. What shall we do to-morrow?
"What shall we ever do?"
　　　　　　　　　　　The hot water at ten.
And if it rains, a closed car at four.
And we shall play a game of chess,
Pressing lidless eyes and waiting for a knock upon the door.

When Lil's husband got demobbed, I said—
I didn't mince my words, I said to her myself,
HURRY UP PLEASE ITS TIME
Now Albert's coming back, make yourself a bit smart.
He'll want to know what you done with that money he gave you
To get yourself some teeth. He did, I was there.
You have them all out, Lil, and get a nice set,
He said, I swear, I can't bear to look at you.
And no more can't I, I said, and think of poor Albert,
He's been in the army four years, he wants a good time,
And if you don't give it him, there's others will, I said.
Oh is there, she said. Something o' that, I said.
Then I'll know who to thank, she said, and give me a straight look.
HURRY UP PLEASE ITS TIME
If you don't like it you can get on with it, I said.
Others can pick and choose if you can't.
But if Albert makes off, it won't be for lack of telling.
You ought to be ashamed, I said, to look so antique.
(And her only thirty-one.)
I can't help it, she said, pulling a long face,
It's them pills I took, to bring it off, she said.
(She's had five already, and nearly died of young George.)
The chemist said it would be all right, but I've never been the same.
You are a proper fool, I said.
Well, if Albert won't leave you alone, there it is, I said,
What you get married for if you don't want children?
HURRY UP PLEASE ITS TIME
Well, that Sunday Albert was home, they had a hot gammon,
And they asked me in to dinner, to get the beauty of it hot—
HURRY UP PLEASE ITS TIME
HURRY UP PLEASE ITS TIME
Goonight Bill. Goonight Lou. Goonight May. Goonight.

Ta ta. Goonight. Goonight.

Good night, ladies, good night, sweet ladies, good night,
  good night.

III. THE FIRE SERMON

The river's tent is broken: the last fingers of leaf
Clutch and sink into the wet bank. The wind
Crosses the brown land, unheard. The nymphs are departed.
Sweet Thames, run softly, till I end my song.
The river bears no empty bottles, sandwich papers,
Silk handkerchiefs, cardboard boxes, cigarette ends
Or other testimony of summer nights. The nymphs are departed.
And their friends, the loitering heirs of city directors;
Departed, have left no addresses.
By the waters of Leman I sat down and wept . . .
Sweet Thames, run softly till I end my song,
Sweet Thames, run softly, for I speak not loud or long.
But at my back in a cold blast I hear
The rattle of the bones, and chuckle spread from ear to ear.
A rat crept softly through the vegetation
Dragging its slimy belly on the bank
While I was fishing in the dull canal
On a winter evening round behind the gashouse
Musing upon the king my brother's wreck
And on the king my father's death before him.
White bodies naked on the low damp ground
And bones cast in a little low dry garret,
Rattled by the rat's foot only, year to year.
But at my back from time to time I hear
The sound of horns and motors, which shall bring
Sweeney to Mrs. Porter in the spring.
O the moon shone bright on Mrs. Porter

And on her daughter
They wash their feet in soda water
Et O ces voix d'enfants, chantant dans la coupole!

 Twit twit twit
Jug jug jug jug jug jug
So rudely forc'd.
Tercu

 Unreal City
Under the brown fog of a winter noon
Mr. Eugenides, the Smyrna merchant
Unshaven, with a pocket full of currants
C.i.f. London: documents at sight,
Asked me in demotic French
To luncheon at the Cannon Street Hotel
Followed by a weekend at the Metropole.

 At the violet hour, when the eyes and back
Turn upward from the desk, when the human engine waits
Like a taxi throbbing waiting,
I Tiresias, though blind, throbbing between two lives,
Old man with wrinkled female breasts, can see
At the violet hour, the evening hour that strives
Homeward, and brings the sailor home from sea,
The typist home at teatime, clears her breakfast, lights
Her stove, and lays out food in tins.
Out of the window perilously spread
Her drying combinations touched by the sun's last rays.
On the divan are piled (at night her bed)
Stockings, slippers, camisoles, and stays.
I Tiresias, old man with wrinkled dugs
Perceived the scene, and foretold the rest—

I too awaited the expected guest.
He, the young man carbuncular, arrives,
A small house agent's clerk, with one bold stare,
One of the low on whom assurance sits
As a silk hat on a Bradford millionaire.
The time is now propitious, as he guesses,
The meal is ended, she is bored and tired,
Endeavours to engage her in caresses
Which still are unreproved, if undesired.
Flushed and decided, he assaults at once;
Exploring hands encounter no defence;
His vanity requires no response,
And makes a welcome of indifference.
(And I Tiresias have foresuffered all
Enacted on this same divan or bed;
I who have sat by Thebes below the wall
And walked among the lowest of the dead.)
Bestows one final patronising kiss,
And gropes his way, finding the stairs unlit . . .

   She turns and looks a moment in the glass,
Hardly aware of her departed lover;
Her brain allows one half-formed thought to pass:
"Well now that's done: and I'm glad it's over."
When lovely woman stoops to folly and
Paces about her room again, alone,
She smoothes her hair with automatic hand,
And puts a record on the gramophone.

"This music crept by me upon the waters"
And along the Strand, up Queen Victoria Street.
O City city, I can sometimes hear
Beside a public bar in Lower Thames Street,
The pleasant whining of a mandoline
And a clatter and a chatter from within
Where fishmen lounge at noon: where the walls
Of Magnus Martyr hold
Inexplicable splendour of Ionian white and gold.

    The river sweats
    Oil and tar
    The barges drift
    With the turning tide
    Red sails
    Wide
    To leeward, swing on the heavy spar.
    The barges wash
    Drifting logs
    Down Greenwich reach
    Past the Isle of Dogs.
              Weialala leia
              Wallala leialala

    Elizabeth and Leicester
    Beating oars
    The stern was formed
    A gilded shell
    Red and gold
    The brisk swell
    Rippled both shores
    Southwest wind
    Carried down stream

The peal of bells
White towers
      Weialala leia
      Wallala leialala

  "Trams and dusty trees.
Highbury bore me. Richmond and Kew
Undid me. By Richmond I raised my knees
Supine on the floor of a narrow canoe."

  "My feet are at Moorgate, and my heart
Under my feet. After the event
He wept. He promised 'a new start.'
I made no comment. What should I resent?"

  "On Margate Sands.
I can connect
Nothing with nothing.
The broken fingernails of dirty hands.
My people humble people who expect
Nothing."
          la la

  To Carthage then I came

  Burning burning burning burning
O Lord Thou pluckest me out
O Lord Thou pluckest

burning

IV. DEATH BY WATER

Phlebas the Phoenician, a fortnight dead,
Forgot the cry of gulls, and the deep sea swell
And the profit and loss.
                 A current under sea
Picked his bones in whispers. As he rose and fell
He passed the stages of his age and youth
Entering the whirlpool.
                 Gentile or Jew
O you who turn the wheel and look to windward,
Consider Phlebas, who was once handsome and tall as you.

V. WHAT THE THUNDER SAID

After the torchlight red on sweaty faces
After the frosty silence in the gardens
After the agony in stony places
The shouting and the crying
Prison and palace and reverberation
Of thunder of spring over distant mountains
He who was living is now dead
We who were living are now dying
With a little patience

     Here is no water but only rock
Rock and no water and the sandy road
The road winding above among the mountains
Which are mountains of rock without water
If there were water we should stop and drink
Amongst the rock one cannot stop or think
Sweat is dry and feet are in the sand
If there were only water amongst the rock

Dead mountain mouth of carious teeth that cannot spit
Here one can neither stand nor lie nor sit
There is not even silence in the mountains
But dry sterile thunder without rain
There is not even solitude in the mountains
But red sullen faces sneer and snarl
From doors a mudcracked houses
                                        If there were water

    And no rock
    If there were rock
    And also water
    And water
    A spring
    A pool among the rock
    If there were the sound of water only
    Not the cicada
    And dry grass singing
    But sound of water over a rock
    Where the hermit thrush sings in the pine trees
    Drip drop drip drop drop drop drop
    But there is no water

    Who is the third who walks always beside you?
When I count, there are only you and I together
But when I look ahead up the white road
There is always another one walking beside you
Gliding wrapt in a brown mantle, hooded
I do not know whether a man or a woman
—But who is that on the other side of you?

    What is that sound high in the air
Murmur of maternal lamentation
Who are those hooded hordes swarming

Over endless plains, stumbling in cracked earth
Ringed by the flat horizon only
What is the city over the mountains
Cracks and reforms and bursts in the violet air
Falling towers
Jerusalem Athens Alexandria
Vienna London
Unreal

A woman drew her long black hair out tight
And fiddled whisper music on those strings
And bats with baby faces in the violet light
Whistled, and beat their wings
And crawled head downward down a blackened wall
And upside down in air were towers
Tolling reminiscent bells, that kept the hours
And voices singing out of empty cisterns and exhausted wells.

In this decayed hole among the mountains
In the faint moonlight, the grass is singing
Over the tumbled graves, about the chapel
There is the empty chapel, only the wind's home.
It has no windows, and the door swings,
Dry bones can harm no one.
Only a cock stood on the rooftree
Co co rico co co rico
In a flash of lightning. Then a damp gust
Bringing rain

Ganga was sunken, and the limp leaves
Waited for rain, while the black clouds
Gathered far distant, over Himavant.
The jungle crouched, humped in silence.

Then spoke the thunder
DA
Datta: what have we given?
My friend, blood shaking my heart
The awful daring of a moment's surrender
Which an age of prudence can never retract
By this, and this only, we have existed
Which is not to be found in our obituaries
Or in memories draped by the beneficent spider
Or under seals broken by the lean solicitor
In our empty rooms
DA
Dayadhvam: I have heard the key
Turn in the door once and turn once only
We think of the key, each in his prison
Thinking of the key, each confirms a prison
Only at nightfall, aethereal rumours
Revive for a moment a broken Coriolanus
DA
Damyata: The boat responded
Gaily, to the hand expert with sail and oar
The sea was calm, your heart would have responded
Gaily, when invited, beating obedient
To controlling hands

                      I sat upon the shore
Fishing, with the arid plain behind me
Shall I at least set my lands in order?
London Bridge is falling down falling down falling down
Poi s'ascose nel foco che gli affina
Quando fiam uli chelidon—O swallow swallow
Le Prince d'Aquitaine à la tour abolie
These fragments I have shored against my ruins

Why then Ile fit you. Hieronymo's mad againe.

Datta. Dayadhvam. Damyata.

Shantih shantih shantih

Notes On *The Waste Land*

Not only the title, but the plan and a good deal of the incidental symbolism of the poem were suggested by Miss Jessie L. Weston's book on the Grail legend: *From Ritual to Romance* (Cambridge). Indeed, so deeply am I indebted, Miss Weston's book will elucidate the difficulties of the poem much better than my notes can do; and I recommend it (apart from the great interest of the book itself) to any who think such elucidation of the poem worth the trouble. To another work of anthropology I am indebted in general, one which has influenced our generation profoundly; I mean *The Golden Bough*; I have used especially the two volumes *Adonis, Attis, Osiris*. Anyone who is acquainted with these works will immediately recognise in the poem certain references to vegetation ceremonies.

I. THE BURIAL OF THE DEAD

Line 20. Cf. Ezekiel II, i.

23. Cf. Ecclesiastes XII, v.

31. V. Tristan und Isolde, I, verses 5–8.

42. Id. III, verse 24.

46. I am not familiar with the exact constitution of the Tarot pack of cards, from which I have obviously departed to suit my own convenience. The Hanged Man, a member of the traditional pack, fits my purpose in two ways: because he is associated in my mind with the Hanged God of Frazer, and because I associate him with the hooded figure in the passage of the disciples to Emmaus in Part V. The Phoenician Sailor and the Merchant appear later; also the "crowds of people," and Death by Water is executed in Part IV. The Man with Three Staves (an authentic member of the Tarot pack) I associate, quite arbitrarily, with the Fisher King himself.

60. Cf. Baudelaire:

"Fourmillante cité, cité pleine de rêves,

"Où le spectre en plein jour raccroche le passant."

63. Cf. Inferno III, 55–57:

"si lunga tratta

di gente, ch'io non avrei mai creduto

che morte tanta n'avesse disfatta."

64. Cf. Inferno IV, 25–27:

"Quivi, secondo che per ascoltare,

"non avea pianto, ma' che di sospiri,

"che l'aura eterna facevan tremare."

68. A phenomenon which I have often noticed.

74. Cf. the Dirge in Webster's *White Devil*.

76. V. Baudelaire, Preface to *Fleurs du Mal*.

II. A GAME OF CHESS

77. Cf. *Antony and Cleopatra*, II, ii, l. 190.

92. Laquearia. V. *Aeneid,* I, 726:

dependent lychni laquearibus aureis incensi, et noctem flammis funalia vincunt.

98. Sylvan scene. V. Milton, *Paradise Lost,* IV, 140.

99. V. Ovid, *Metamorphoses,* VI, Philomela.

100. Cf. Part III, l. 204.

115. Cf. Part III, l. 195.

118. Cf. Webster: "Is the wind in that door still?"

126. Cf. Part I, l. 37, 48.

138. Cf. the game of chess in Middleton's *Women beware Women*.

III. THE FIRE SERMON

176. V. Spenser, *Prothalamion*.

192. Cf. *The Tempest,* I, ii.

196. Cf. Marvell, *To His Coy Mistress*.

197. Cf. Day, *Parliament of Bees:*

> "When of the sudden, listening, you shall hear,
>
> "A noise of horns and hunting, which shall bring
>
> "Actaeon to Diana in the spring,
>
> "Where all shall see her naked skin . . ."

199. I do not know the origin of the ballad from which these lines are taken: it was reported to me from Sydney, Australia.

202. V. Verlaine, *Parsifal.*

210. The currants were quoted at a price "carriage and insurance free to London"; and the Bill of Lading etc. were to be handed to the buyer upon payment of the sight draft.

218. Tiresias, although a mere spectator and not indeed a "character," is yet the most important personage in the poem, uniting all the rest. Just as the one-eyed merchant, seller of currants, melts into the Phoenician Sailor, and the latter is not wholly distinct from Ferdinand Prince of Naples, so all the women are one woman, and the two sexes meet in Tiresias. What Tiresias *sees,* in fact, is the substance of the poem. The whole passage from Ovid is of great anthropological interest:

> '. . . Cum Iunone iocos et maior vestra profecto est
>
> Quam, quae contingit maribus,' dixisse, 'voluptas.'
>
> Illa negat; placuit quae sit sententia docti
>
> Quaerere Tiresiae: venus huic erat utraque nota.
>
> Nam duo magnorum viridi cocuntia silva
>
> Corpora serpentum baculi violaverat ictu
>
> Deque viro factus, mirabile, femina septem
>
> Egerat autumnos: octavo rursus eosdem
>
> Vidit et 'est vestrae si tanta potentia plagae,'
>
> Dixit 'ut auctoris sortem in contraria mutet,
>
> Nunc quoque vos feriam!' percussis anguibus isdem
>
> Forma prior rediit genetivaque venit imago.
>
> Arbiter hic igitur sumptus de lite iocosa
>
> Dicta Iovis firmat; gravius Saturnia iusto
>
> Nec pro materia fertur doluisse suique

Iudicis aeterna damnavit lumina nocte,

At pater omnipotens (neque enim licet inrita cuiquam

Facta dei fecisse deo) pro lumine adempto

Scire futura dedit poenamque levavit honore.

221. This may not appear as exact as Sappho's lines, but I had in mind the "longshore" or "dory" fisherman, who returns at nightfall.

253. V. Goldsmith, the song in *The Vicar of Wakefield*.

257. V. *The Tempest*, as above.

264. The interior of St. Magnus Martyr is to my mind one of the finest among Wren's interiors. See *The Proposed Demolition of Nineteen City Churches:* (P. S. King & Son, Ltd.).

266. The Song of the (three) Thames-daughters begins here. From line 292 to 306 inclusive they speak in turn. V. *Götterdämmerung*, III, i: the Rhine daughters.

279. V. Froude, *Elizabeth*, Vol. I, ch. iv, letter of De Quadra to Philip of Spain: "In the afternoon we were in a barge, watching the games on the river. (The queen) was alone with Lord Robert and myself on the poop, when they began to talk nonsense, and went so far that Lord Robert at last said, as I was on the spot there was no reason why they should not be married if the queen pleased."

293. Cf. *Purgatorio*, V, 133:

"Ricorditi di me, che son la Pia;

"Siena mi fe', disfecemi Maremma."

307. V. St. Augustine's *Confessions:* "to Carthage then I came, where a cauldron of unholy loves sang all about mine ears."

308. The complete text of the Buddha's Fire Sermon (which corresponds in importance to the Sermon on the Mount) from which these words are taken, will be found translated in the late Henry Clarke Warren's *Buddhism in Translation* (Harvard Oriental Series). Mr. Warren was one of the great pioneers of Buddhist studies in the Occident.

309. From St. Augustine's *Confessions* again. The collocation of these two representatives of eastern and western asceticism, as the culmination of this part of the poem, is not an accident.

V. WHAT THE THUNDER SAID

In the first part of Part V three themes are employed: the journey to Emmaus, the approach to the Chapel Perilous (see Miss Weston's book) and the present decay of eastern Europe.

357. This is *Turdus aonalaschkae pallasii*, the hermit-thrush which I have heard in Quebec Province. Chapman says (*Handbook of Birds of Eastern North America*) "it is most at home in secluded woodland and thickety retreats. . . . Its notes are not remarkable for variety or volume, but in purity and sweetness of tone and exquisite modulation they are unequalled." Its "water-dripping song" is justly celebrated.

360. The following lines were stimulated by the account of one of the Antarctic expeditions (I forget which, but I think one of Shackleton's): it was related that the party of explorers, at the extremity of their strength, had the constant delusion that there was *one more member* than could actually be counted.

367–77. Cf. Hermann Hesse, *Blick ins Chaos:* "Schon ist halb Europa, schon ist zumindest der halbe Osten Europas auf dem Wege zum Chaos, fährt betrunken im heiligem Wahn am Abgrund entlang und singt dazu, singt betrunken und hymnisch wie Dmitri Karamasoff sang. Ueber diese Lieder lacht der Bürger beleidigt, der Heilige und Scher hört sie mit Tränen."

402. "Datta, dayadhvam, damyata" (Give, sympathise, control). The fable of the meaning of the Thunder is found in the *Brihadaranyaka—Upanishad*, 5, 1. A translation is found in Deussen's *Sechzig Upanishads des Veda,* p. 489.

408. Cf. Webster, *The White Devil,* V, vi:

> ". . . they'll remarry
>
> Ere the worm pierce your winding-sheet, ere the spider
>
> Make a thin curtain for your epitaphs."

412. Cf. *Inferno,* XXXIII, 46:

> "ed io sentii chiavar l'uscio di sotto
>
> all'orribile torre."

Also F. H. Bradley, *Appearance and Reality,* p. 346.

'My external sensations are no less private to myself than are my thoughts or my feelings. In either case my experience falls within my own circle, a circle closed on the outside; and, with all its elements alike, every sphere is opaque to the others which surround it. . . . In brief, regarded as an existence which appears in a soul, the whole world for each is peculiar and private to that soul."

425. V. Weston: *From Ritual to Romance;* chapter on the Fisher King.

428. V. *Purgatorio,* XXVI, 148.

> " 'Ara vos prec per aquella valor
>
> 'que vos guida al som de l'escalina,
>
> 'sovegna vos a temps de ma dolor.'
>
> Poi s'ascose nel foco che gli affina."

429. V. *Pervigilium Veneris.* Cf. Philomela in Parts II and III.

430. V. Gerard de Nerval, Sonnet *El Desdichado.*

432. V. Kyd's *Spanish Tragedy.*

434. Shantih. Repeated as here, a formal ending to an Upanishad. "The Peace which passeth understanding" is our equivalent to this word.

EDNA ST. VINCENT MILLAY
(1892–1950)

Edna St. Vincent Millay was raised with her two sisters by a single mother, who had left her husband when Edna was eight years old. A scholarship to Vassar introduced her to a circle of literary women which she enthusiastically joined, forming several romantic relationships. Eventually she became one of the leaders of a bohemian artistic group in postwar Greenwich Village. Her aggressively hedonistic lifestyle and the lyrical quality of her writing should not detract from the importance of her work, which casts a frankly sardonic eye on what the rest of the world considers to be respectable and appropriate.

Perhaps her most famous poem, this brief verse typifies the traditional image of the brilliant poet burning out in a few moments of hedonism and creativity. The poet did not, however, expire as fast as some of her peers, living to the age of fifty-eight.

First Fig

My candle burns at both ends;
 It will not last the night;
But ah, my foes, and oh, my friends—
 It gives a lovely light!

Using the traditional sonnet form, Millay here offers a variation on the presumed romantic weakness of women, distinguishing the momentary passion of the flesh from any lasting commitment. This poem is virtually a manifesto for the concept of meaningless sex.

I, Being Born a Woman and Distressed

I, being born a woman and distressed
By all the needs and notions of my kind,
Am urged by your propinquity to find
Your person fair, and feel a certain zest
To bear your body's weight upon my breast:
So subtly is the fume of life designed,
To clarify the pulse and cloud the mind,
And leave me once again undone, possessed.
Think not for this, however, the poor treason
Of my stout blood against my staggering brain,
I shall remember you with love, or season
My scorn with pity,—let me make it plain:
I find this frenzy insufficient reason
For conversation when we meet again.

Again articulating an unromantic vision of a romantic subject, Millay considers April not, as Eliot would have it in *The Waste Land*, "the cruelest month," but rather an irrational symbol of rebirth.

Spring

To what purpose, April, do you return again?
Beauty is not enough.
You can no longer quiet me with the redness
Of little leaves opening stickily.
I know what I know.
The sun is hot on my neck as I observe
The spikes of the crocus.
The smell of the earth is good.
It is apparent that there is no death.
But what does that signify?
Not only under ground are the brains of men
Eaten by maggots.
Life in itself
Is nothing,
An empty cup, a flight of uncarpeted stairs.
It is not enough that yearly, down this hill,
April
Comes like an idiot, babbling and strewing flowers.

This genuinely romantic recollection is also a love letter to a New York City of golden memory.

Recuerdo

We were very tired, we were very merry—
We had gone back and forth all night on the ferry.
It was bare and bright, and smelled like a stable—
But we looked into a fire, we leaned across a table,
We lay on a hill-top underneath the moon;
And the whistles kept blowing, and the dawn came soon.

We were very tired, we were very merry—
We had gone back and forth all night on the ferry;
And you ate an apple, and I ate a pear,
From a dozen of each we had bought somewhere;
And the sky went wan, and the wind came cold,
And the sun rose dripping, a bucketful of gold.

We were very tired, we were very merry,
We had gone back and forth all night on the ferry.
We hailed, "Good morrow, mother!" to a shawl-covered head,
And bought a morning paper, which neither of us read;
And she wept, "God bless you!" for the apples and the pears,
And we gave her all our money but our subway fares.

A recapitulation of the sentiment expressed in "First Fig," above, this poem also prizes a brief, ecstatic moment above a drab stability, indicating that brevity of existence is an inherent element of its preciousness. In this Millay's esthetic resembles the Japanese concept of beauty as inherently ephemeral, like a falling cherry blossom.

Second Fig

Safe upon the solid rock the ugly houses stand:
Come and see my shining palace built upon the sand!

DOROTHY PARKER

(1893–1967)

Dorothy Parker spent all of her writing life battling against sentimentality. A celebrated wit in an era of great wit, she was one of the stars of the legendary Algonquin Round Table, an informal lunch group of *New Yorker* writers and others that included at various times the humorist Robert Benchley, the dramatists Robert Sherwood and George S. Kaufman, and even occasionally Harpo Marx! Parker was renowned as a prose writer, but her incisive, ironic poetry, written in a recognizably contemporary voice, is what keeps her reputation alive.

This is probably Parker's most familiar poem, typically mordant and witty, but with a dark and almost palpable underlying theme of hopelessness. Parker herself attempted suicide on a number of occasions.

Résumé

Razors pain you;
Rivers are damp;
Acids stain you;
And drugs cause cramp.
Guns aren't lawful;
Nooses give;
Gas smells awful;
You might as well live.

E. E. CUMMINGS

(1894–1962)

Cummings often used typography to help create an effect for his poetry, perhaps influenced by his association with artists like Picasso and Gertrude Stein during the time he spent in Paris after World War I. This style is very evident in the poem below. Buffalo Bill Cody was a famous figure of what was known as the Wild West, who in later life presided over a popular show that featured both the celebrated Little Miss Sure Shot, Annie Oakley, and the great Sioux chief Sitting Bull.

Buffalo Bill's

Buffalo Bill's
defunct
     who used to
     ride a watersmooth-silver
                    stallion
and break onetwothreefourfive pigeonsjustlikethat
                              Jesus

he was a handsome man
                   and what i want to know is
how do you like your blueeyed boy
Mister Death

Cummings was known for a sometimes sentimental romanticism. The poem below presents a childlike image of spring that yet features a rather domesticated paganism in the figure of the goat-footed balloon man.

In Just-

in Just-
spring   when the world is mud-
luscious the little
lame balloonman

whistles   far   and wee

and eddieandbill come
running from marbles and
piracies and it's
spring

when the world is puddle-wonderful

the queer
old balloonman whistles
far   and   wee
and bettyandisbel come dancing

from hop-scotch and jump-rope and

it's
spring
and
   the
      goat-footed

balloonMan   whistles
far
and
wee

HART CRANE
(1899–1932)

The brief life of Hart Crane seems almost a metaphor for romantic poetry. Brilliant, tortured, untutored but almost instinctively and ecstatically creative, Crane sampled virtually every modern American and European poetic style. In his work can be found a Whitman-like passionate identification with the American spirit, an Eliot-like concern with the effect of industrialization on modern life, and a fascination with the kind of images found in the work of Pound, Stevens, Williams, and Cummings. His masterwork takes the Brooklyn Bridge as a symbol with many meanings; the poem below is just one example of how Crane used it as a unifying principle. Crane died a suicide, jumping off the deck of an ocean liner. His body was never found.

Proem: To Brooklyn Bridge from *The Bridge*

How many dawns, chill from his rippling rest
The seagull's wings shall dip and pivot him,
Shedding white rings of tumult, building high
Over the chained bay waters Liberty—

Then, with inviolate curve, forsake our eyes
As apparitional as sails that cross
Some page of figures to be filed away;
—Till elevators drop us from our day . . .

I think of cinemas, panoramic sleights
With multitudes bent toward some flashing scene
Never disclosed, but hastened to again,
Foretold to other eyes on the same screen;

And Thee, across the harbor, silver-paced
As though the sun took step of thee, yet left
Some motion ever unspent in thy stride—
Implicitly thy freedom staying thee!

Out of some subway scuttle, cell or loft
A bedlamite speeds to thy parapets,
Tilting there momently, shrill shirt ballooning,
A jest falls from the speechless caravan.

Down Wall, from girder into street noon leaks,
A rip-tooth of the sky's acetylene,
All afternoon the cloud-flown derricks turn . . .
Thy cables breathe the North Atlantic still.

And obscure as that heaven of the Jews,
Thy guerdon . . . Accolade thou dost bestow
Of anonymity time cannot raise:
Vibrant reprieve and pardon thou dost show.

O harp and altar, of the fury fused,
(How could mere toil align thy choiring strings!)
Terrific threshold of the prophet's pledge,
Prayer of pariah, and the lover's cry—

Again the traffic lights that skim thy swift
Unfractioned idiom, immaculate sigh of stars,
Beading thy path—condense eternity:
And we have seen night lifted in thine arms.

Under thy shadow by the piers I waited;
Only in darkness is thy shadow clear.
The City's fiery parcels all undone,
Already snow submerges an iron year . . .

O Sleepless as the river under thee,
Vaulting the sea, the prairies' dreaming sod,
Unto us lowliest sometime sweep, descend
And of the curveship lend a myth to God.

LANGSTON HUGHES

(1902–1967)

Langston Hughes became interested in poetry at an early age; among his first influences were Whitman and Sandburg. As he matured as a poet, he became more concerned with writing as a black man, feeling that to do otherwise was, in his words, to "surrender racial pride in the name of a false integration." His later work was influenced by jazz in its tempo and meter.

The image of the hope of African Americans for a better life drying up like a raisin in the sun has become iconic; it was used as the title of a notable play by Lorraine Hansberry. The implied explosion at the end of the poem prefigures the rhetoric of the Black Power movement of the late 1960s.

Dream Deferred

What happens to a dream deferred?

Does it dry up
like a raisin in the sun?
Or fester like a sore—
And then run?
Does it stink like rotten meat?
Or crust and sugar over—
like a syrupy sweet?

Maybe it just sags
like a heavy load.

Or does it explode?

Hughes's gift for evoking an authentic voice in his poetry is powerfully expressed in this dramatic monologue.

Mother to Son

Well, son, I'll tell you:
Life for me ain't been no crystal stair.
It's had tacks in it,
And splinters,
And boards torn up,
And places with no carpet on the floor—
Bare.
But all the time
I'se been a-climbin' on,
And reachin' landin's,
And turnin' corners,
And sometimes goin' in the dark
Where there ain't been no light.
So boy, don't you turn back.
Don't you set down on the steps.
'Cause you finds it's kinder hard.
Don't you fall now—
For I'se still goin', honey,
I'se still climbin',
And life for me ain't been no crystal stair.

OGDEN NASH
(1902–1971)

The economical wit of Ogden Nash is as satirical and as filled with social commentary as Dorothy Parker's, but much more good natured at its heart. When Nash wrote the poem below, before the beautification of the nation's highways led by Lady Bird Johnson in the 1960s, America's public roads were often lined with commercial advertising. Note the parody of Joyce Kilmer's "Trees" (p. 207) in the first two lines of this poem.

Song of the Open Road

I think that I shall never see
A billboard lovely as a tree.
Perhaps, unless the billboards fall,
I'll never see a tree at all.

This recognition of the power of alcohol as a social lubricant has a surprising impact despite its almost haiku-like brevity.

Reflections on Ice-breaking

Candy
Is dandy
But liquor
Is quicker.

ROBERT JOHNSON

(1911–1938)

The music called "the blues" (probably derived from a common term for depression that goes back at least to Elizabethan times) can be traced back to African rhythms and work songs and church chants of African slaves in the American South. The lyrics generally repeated two lines of four beats each, and then ended with a resolution; the power of this metric form, accompanied by creative guitar playing that generally provided the response in a call-and-response structure, helped fuel the rock 'n' roll revolution of mid-twentieth century. It's interesting to compare a poem like Vachel Lindsay's "The Congo," which attempts to evoke the rhythms of African American music and dance, with the authentic examples below.

Robert Johnson was born in the Mississippi Delta, from which many important blues singers emerged. According to legend he sold his soul to the Devil to gain the power to play the guitar as no one had before. He created a number of important blues lyrics, which he often altered in different performances; below is one version of "Cross Roads Blues," in which the usual three-line verse structure is broken up and doubled.

Cross Roads Blues (Crossroads)

I went to the crossroads,
Fell down on my knees.
I went to the crossroads,
Fell down on my knees.
Asked the Lord above for mercy,
"Save poor Bob if you please."

Standing at the crossroads,
Tried to flag a ride.
Standing at the crossroads,
Tried to flag a ride.
Ain't nobody seemed to know me,
Everybody passed me by.

Standin' at the crossroads babe,
Risin' sun goin' down.
Standin' at the crossroads babe,
Risin' sun goin' down.
I believe to my soul now,
Poor Bob is sinkin' down.

You can run, you can run,
Tell my friend-boy Willie Brown.
You can run, you can run,
Tell my friend-boy Willie Brown.
And I'm standing at the crossroads,
I believe I'm sinking down.

TRADITIONAL

(1928)

In 1895 a young man named William Lyons was shot in a St. Louis saloon after grabbing a man's hat off his head. The man, named Lee Shelton, was known as Stag Lee, and he was reported at the time to have coolly taken back his hat after shooting Lyons, and then walked out of the saloon. From this episode the colorful story of Stagger Lee emerged. Many verses describing what became a legendary encounter were created over the decades, sometimes sung and sometimes recited to an audience. In some versions Stagger Lee was executed for his crime, but when he went to hell even the Devil was frightened of him! The history of "Stagger Lee," which became a popular rock 'n' roll song in the mid-twentieth century, is a classic example of how the oral tradition can shape reality into art. Mississippi John Hurt, who recorded one version of this lyric eighty years ago, was himself a legendary Delta blues singer who, after living for many years in obscurity, was rediscovered in the 1960s, as the folk music revival of that period was nearing its peak.

Stagger Lee lyrics recorded by Mississippi John Hurt

Po-lice officer, how can it be?
You can 'rest everybody but cruel Stagolee
That bad man, oh cruel Stagolee.

Billy DeLyon told Stagolee, "Please don't take my life
I got two little babes and a darling, loving wife."
That bad man, oh cruel Stagolee.

"What'd I care about your two little babes and darling, loving wife?
You done stole my Stetson hat, I'm bound to take your life."
That bad man, oh cruel Stagolee.

Boom boom, boom boom,
Went the forty-four.
Well when I spied Billy DeLyon,
He's lyin' down on the floor.
That bad man, oh cruel Stagolee.

Gentlemens of the Jury,
What you think of that?
Stagolee killed Billy DeLyon
'Bout a five-dollar Stetson hat.
That bad man, oh cruel Stagolee.

Standin' on the gallows, head way up high.
At twelve o'clock, they killed him,
They's all glad to see him die.
That bad man, oh cruel Stagolee.

ELIZABETH BISHOP

(1911–1979)

The degree to which poetry is affected by a poet's personal experience is difficult to determine, and the validity of such a connection is a controversial critical question. But to the extent that poetry is autobiographical the connection is inherent, and Bishop, despite warm friendships with such poets as Robert Lowell and especially Marianne Moore, who helped persuade her to make poetry her vocation, lived what can only be called an unhappy life (her one true love, a Brazilian woman who was her nurse after Bishop fell sick on a visit to South America, later killed herself in a state of clinical depression). Despite her sorrows, Bishop was a brilliant poetic technician, and even when she wrote of her personal concerns, they were transfigured by her creative genius, as in the poem below (the repetitive verse form is known as a villanelle). She is certainly one of the outstanding American poets of the twentieth century.

One Art

The art of losing isn't hard to master;
so many things seem filled with the intent
to be lost that their loss is no disaster.

Lose something every day. Accept the fluster
of lost door keys, the hour badly spent.
The art of losing isn't hard to master.

Then practice losing farther, losing faster:
places, and names, and where it was you meant
to travel. None of these will bring disaster.

I lost my mother's watch. And look! my last, or
next-to-last, of three loved houses went.
The art of losing isn't hard to master.

I lost two cities, lovely ones. And, vaster,
some realms I owned, two rivers, a continent.
I miss them, but it wasn't a disaster.

—Even losing you (the joking voice, a gesture
I love) I shan't have lied. It's evident
the art of losing's not too hard to master
though it may look like (*Write* it!) like disaster.

WOODY GUTHRIE

(1912–1967)

Woody Guthrie was a wandering troubadour during the Great Depression, writing songs of the Dust Bowl and impoverished migrant workers that ironically became great popular and commercial successes. The verses below have become to some another national anthem, one with a distinctly populist tone.

This Land Is Your Land

Chorus
This land is your land, this land is my land
From California to the New York Island
From the Redwood Forest, to the Gulf Stream waters
This land was made for you and me.

As I went walking that ribbon of highway
I saw above me an endless skyway
I saw below me a golden valley
This land was made for you and me.

Chorus

I roamed and rambled and I followed my footsteps
To the sparkling sands of her diamond deserts
While all around me a voice was sounding
This land was made for you and me.

Chorus

When the sun came shining, and I was strolling
And the wheat fields waving and the dust clouds rolling
A voice was chanting, as the fog was lifting,
This land was made for you and me.

Chorus

As I was walkin'—I saw a sign there
And that sign said 'private property'
But on the other side . . . . it didn't say nothin!
Now that side was made for you and me!

Chorus

In the squares of the city, in the shadow of the steeple
Near the relief office, I'd seen my people
As they stood there hungry, I stood there asking,
Is this land made for you and me?

Chorus

RANDALL JARRELL
(1914–1965)

This brief poem condenses a human life with an almost unbearable intensity from birth to a brief awakening to a horrifying termination. The ball turret on a B-17 bomber was a small plexiglass bubble on the bottom of the plane in which a man, usually of slight build, sat crouched in a virtual fetal position with an almost 360-degree exposure to any attacking planes, while manning two .50 caliber machine guns.

The Death of the Ball Turret Gunner

From my mother's sleep I fell into the State,
And I hunched in its belly till my wet fur froze.
Six miles from earth, loosed from its dream of life,
I woke to black flak and the nightmare fighters.
When I died they washed me out of the turret with a hose.

ROBERT LOWELL

(1917–1977)

Late in the nineteenth century, a bronze monument was erected on the Boston Common, created by the sculptor Augustus Saint-Gaudens, to honor Robert Gould Shaw, the white leader of a Massachusetts regiment made up of free black men, many of whom had died in an assault on a Confederate battery in South Carolina in 1863. (The story of Shaw and his regiment was dramatized in the motion picture *Glory.*) At the time Lowell wrote this poem, in the mid-1960s, the sculpture had been removed temporarily to permit the construction of a new aquarium and an underground parking garage (it has since been restored to its place of honor, in front of the Massachusetts State House), and Lowell seems to contrast the idealism of the men portrayed on the monument with the materialistic culture that he saw around him as he wrote. On the sculpture are engraved the words *Relinquit omnia servare rem publicam*, meaning he (Shaw) left behind everything to serve the republic; in the poem's epigraph, Lowell makes the verb plural, to represent not only Shaw but his brave soldiers: They gave everything to serve the republic.

For the Union Dead

"Relinquunt omnia servare rem publicam."

The old South Boston Aquarium stands
in a Sahara of snow now. Its broken windows are boarded.
The bronze weathervane cod has lost half its scales.
The airy tanks are dry.

Once my nose crawled like a snail on the glass;
my hand tingled
to burst the bubbles,
drifting from the noses of the cowed, compliant fish.

My hand draws back. I often sigh still
for the dark downward and vegetating kingdom
of the fish and reptile. One morning last March,
I pressed against the new barbed and galvanized

fence on the Boston Common. Behind their cage,
yellow dinosaur steamshovels were grunting
as they cropped up tons of mush and grass
to gouge their underworld garage.

Parking lots luxuriate like civic
sandpiles in the heart of Boston.
A girdle of orange, Puritan-pumpkin colored girders
braces the tingling Statehouse,

shaking over the excavations, as it faces Colonel Shaw
and his bell-cheeked Negro infantry
on St. Gaudens' shaking Civil War relief,
propped by a plank splint against the garage's earthquake.

Two months after marching through Boston,
half the regiment was dead;
at the dedication,
William James could almost hear the bronze Negroes breathe.

The monument sticks like a fishbone
in the city's throat.
Its Colonel is as lean
as a compass-needle.

He has an angry wrenlike vigilance,
a greyhound's gentle tautness;
he seems to wince at pleasure,
and suffocate for privacy.

He is out of bounds. He rejoices in man's lovely,
peculiar power to choose life and die—
when he leads his black soldiers to death,
he cannot bend his back.

On a thousand small town New England greens,
the old white churches hold their air
of sparse, sincere rebellion; frayed flags
quilt the graveyards of the Grand Army of the Republic

The stone statues of the abstract Union Soldier
grow slimmer and younger each year—
wasp-waisted, they doze over muskets,
and muse through their sideburns . . .

Shaw's father wanted no monument
except the ditch,
where his son's body was thrown
and lost with his "niggers."

The ditch is nearer.
There are no statues for the last war here;
on Boylston Street, a commercial photograph
showed Hiroshima boiling

over a Mosler Safe, the "Rock of Ages"
that survived the blast. Space is nearer.
When I crouch to my television set,
the drained faces of Negro school-children rise like balloons.

Colonel Shaw
'is riding on his bubble,
he waits
for the blesséd break.

The Aquarium is gone. Everywhere,
giant finned cars nose forward like fish;
a savage servility
slides by on grease.

GWENDOLYN BROOKS
(1917–2000)

Here is what Gwendolyn Brooks herself wrote about how she felt her most famous poem should be recited: "First of all, let me tell you how that's supposed to be said, because there's a reason why I set it out as I did. These are people who are essentially saying, 'Kilroy is here. We are.' But they're a little uncertain of the strength of their identity. The 'We'—you're supposed to stop after the 'we' and think about validity; of course, there's no way for you to tell whether it should be said softly or not, I suppose, but I say it rather softly because I want to represent their basic uncertainty."

We Real Cool
THE POOL PLAYERS.
SEVEN AT THE GOLDEN SHOVEL.

We real cool. We
Left school. We

Lurk late. We
Strike straight. We

Sing sin. We
Thin gin. We

Jazz June. We
Die soon.

ATTRIBUTED TO PVT. WILLIE DUCKWORTH

(CA. 1944)

According to a contemporary account, one day in 1944 an African American enlisted man was marching a company of recruits at Fort Slocum, New York, when he decided to liven up the routine of "left, right; left, right" with a series of call-and-response chants. The commanding officer of the post, a songwriter in civilian life, helped adapt the chant into a song that was recorded by a number of well-known vocalists. Meanwhile, as the soldiers from Fort Slocum were reassigned, variations of the Duckworth Chant sprang up over the years at military posts around the country and the world, an ongoing example of the vitality of the oral poetic tradition.

Sound Off Marching Cadence Count (derived from the Duckworth Chant)

The heads are up, the chests are out
The arms are swingin' in cadence, count:

> Sound off! (one-two).
> Sound off! (three-four).
> Bring it on down!
> (One, two, three, four—
> One two! Three four!)

Eeny meeny miney moe
Let's go back and count some mo'

Sound off! (one-two).
Sound off! (three-four).
Bring it on down!
(One, two, three, four—
One two! Three four!)

We will march to beat the band
And we'll never bite The Hand

Sound off! (one-two).
Sound off! (three-four).
Bring it on down!
(One, two, three, four—
One two! Three four!)

I had a good home but I left (you're right!)
I had a good home but I left (you're right!)

Jody was there when you left (you're right!)
Jody was there when you left (you're right!)

Sound off! (one-two).
Sound off! (three-four).
Bring it on down!
(One, two, three, four—
One two! Three four!)

It won't get by if it ain't GI
It won't get by if it ain't GI

Sound off! (one-two).
Sound off! (three-four).
Bring it on down!
(One, two, three, four—
One two! Three four!)

If I die in a combat zone
Just box me up and send me home

Sound off! (one-two).
Sound off! (three-four).
Bring it on down!
(One, two, three, four—
One two! Three four!)

I don't mind to take a hike
If I could take along a bike

Sound off! (one-two).
Sound off! (three-four).
Bring it on down!
(One, two, three, four—
One two! Three four!)

I don't mind a bivouac
If I could take along a WAC

Sound off! (one-two).
Sound off! (three-four).
Bring it on down!
(One, two, three, four—
One two! Three four!)

The WACs and WAVEs will win the war
So tell us what we're fighting for

Sound off! (one-two).
Sound off! (three-four).
Bring it on down!
(One, two, three, four—
One two! Three four!)

You had a good job but you left (you're right!)
You had a good job but you left (you're right!)

Sound off! (one-two).
Sound off! (three-four).
Bring it on down!
(One, two, three, four—
One two! Three four!)

Ain't no use in goin' home,
Jody's got your girl and gone.

Sound off! (one-two).
Sound off! (three-four).
Bring it on down!
(One, two, three, four—
One two! Three four!)

The Captain rides in a jeep.
(You're right!)
The Sergeant rides in a truck.
(You're right!)
The General rides in a limousine,
But you're just outta luck!
(You're right!)

Sound off! (one-two).
Sound off! (three-four).
Bring it on down!
(One, two, three, four—
One two! Three four!)

FRANK O'HARA
(1926–1966)

Frank O'Hara was perhaps the most prominent member of the New York School of poets, who attempted to use conversational language to create a kind of intuitive understanding of the significance of a moment or an image. It's not coincidental that O'Hara was also closely associated with contemporary movements in modern art such as abstract expressionism and pop art, which similarly sought to create effects through nonlinear and often commonplace references. In the poem below, the death of the great jazz singer Billie Holliday emerges almost incidentally from a seemingly random accounting of the poet's lunchtime excursion when a chance glimpse of a newspaper headline suddenly realigns the poet's universe and transports him to another time and place.

The Day Lady Died

It is 12:20 in New York a Friday
three days after Bastille day, yes
it is 1959 and I go get a shoeshine
because I will get off the 4:19 in Easthampton
at 7:15 and then go straight to dinner
and I don't know the people who will feed me

I walk up the muggy street beginning to sun
and have a hamburger and a malted and buy
an ugly NEW WORLD WRITING to see what the poets
in Ghana are doing these days
                              I go on to the bank
and Miss Stillwagon (first name Linda I once heard)
doesn't even look up my balance for once in her life
and in the GOLDEN GRIFFIN I get a little Verlaine
for Patsy with drawings by Bonnard although I do
think of Hesiod, trans. Richmond Lattimore or
Brendan Behan's new play or *Le Balcon* or *Les Nègres*
of Genet, but I don't, I stick with Verlaine
after practically going to sleep with quandariness

and for Mike I just stroll into the PARK LANE
Liquor Store and ask for a bottle of Strega and
then I go back where I came from to 6th Avenue
and the tobacconist in the Ziegfeld Theatre and
casually ask for a carton of Gauloises and a carton
of Picayunes, and a NEW YORK POST with her face on it

and I am sweating a lot by now and thinking of
leaning on the john door in the 5 SPOT
while she whispered a song along the keyboard
to Mal Waldron and everyone and I stopped breathing

ALLEN GINSBERG

(1926–1997)

The Beat poet Allen Ginsberg's tribute to his great poetic inspiration is a warm, witty, and poignant meditation on how much America has changed since Whitman first sang the nation's praises.

A Supermarket in California

What thoughts I have of you tonight, Walt Whitman, for I walked down the sidestreets under the trees with a headache self-conscious looking at the full moon.

In my hungry fatigue, and shopping for images, I went into the neon fruit supermarket, dreaming of your enumerations!

What peaches and what penumbras! Whole families shopping at night! Aisles full of husbands! Wives in the avocados, babies in the tomatoes!—and you, García Lorca, what were you doing down by the watermelons?

I saw you, Walt Whitman, childless, lonely old grubber, poking among the meats in the refrigerator and eyeing the grocery boys.

I heard you asking questions of each: Who killed the pork chops? What price bananas? Are you my Angel?

I wandered in and out of the brilliant stacks of cans following you, and followed in my imagination by the store detective.

We strode down the open corridors together in our solitary fancy tasting artichokes, possessing every frozen delicacy, and never passing the cashier.

Where are we going, Walt Whitman? The doors close in an hour. Which way does your beard point tonight?

(I touch your book and dream of our odyssey in the supermarket and feel absurd.)

Will we walk all night through solitary streets? The trees add shade to shade, lights out in the houses, we'll both be lonely.

Will we stroll dreaming of the lost America of love past blue automobiles in driveways, home to our silent cottage?

Ah, dear father, graybeard, lonely old courage-teacher, what America did you have when Charon quit poling his ferry and you got out on a smoking bank and stood watching the boat disappear on the black waters of Lethe?

Berkeley, 1955

SYLVIA PLATH

(1932–1963)

Sylvia Plath lived a short, legendary life. In her passion, her ambition, her urge to self destruction, she became a kind of cautionary beacon to American women at the dawn of what was known in the late 1960s as Women's Liberation. Plath was no traditional feminist, but wrote, in this poem at least, like a kind of avenging Fury, hurling her diatribe not simply at her distant father, who died when she was a child, or her poet-husband Ted Hughes, who went off with another woman, but at a vampiric, Nazi-like image of male domination.

Daddy

You do not do, you do not do
Any more, black shoe
In which I have lived like a foot
For thirty years, poor and white,
Barely daring to breathe or Achoo.

Daddy, I have had to kill you.
You died before I had time—
Marble-heavy, a bag full of God,
Ghastly statue with one gray toe
Big as a Frisco seal

And a head in the freakish Atlantic
Where it pours bean green over blue
In the waters off beautiful Nauset.
I used to pray to recover you.
Ach, du.

In the German tongue, in the Polish town
Scraped flat by the roller
Of wars, wars, wars.
But the name of the town is common.
My Polack friend

Says there are a dozen or two.
So I could never tell where you
Put your foot, your root,
I could never talk to you.
The tongue stuck in my jaw.

It stuck in a barb wire snare.
Ich, ich, ich, ich,
I could hardly speak.
I thought every German was you.
And the language obscene

An engine, an engine
Chuffing me off like a Jew.
A Jew to Dachau, Auschwitz, Belsen.
I began to talk like a Jew.
I think I may well be a Jew.

The snows of Tyrol, the clear beer of Vienna
Are not very pure or true.
With my gypsy ancestress and my weird luck
And my Tarot pack and my Tarot pack
I may be a bit of a Jew.

I have always been scared of *you,*
With your Luftwaffe, your gobbledygoo.
And your neat mustache
And your Aryan eye, bright blue.
Panzer-man, panzer-man, O You—

Not God but a swastika
So black no sky could squeak through.
Every woman adores a Fascist,
The boot in the face, the brute
Brute heart of a brute like you.

You stand at the blackboard, daddy,
In the picture I have of you,
A cleft in your chin instead of your foot
But no less a devil for that, no not
Any less the black man who

Bit my pretty red heart in two.
I was ten when they buried you.
At twenty I tried to die
And get back, back, back to you.
I thought even the bones would do.

But they pulled me out of the sack,
And they stuck me together with glue,
And then I knew what to do.
I made a model of you,
A man in black with a Meinkampf look

And a love of the rack and the screw.
And I said I do, I do.
So daddy, I'm finally through.
The black telephone's off at the root,
The voices just can't worm through.

If I've killed one man, I've killed two—
The vampire who said he was you
And drank my blood for a year,
Seven years, if you want to know.
Daddy, you can lie back now.

There's a stake in your fat black heart
And the villagers never liked you.
They are dancing and stamping on you.
They always *knew* it was you.
Daddy, daddy, you bastard, I'm through.

BILLY COLLINS

(1941–)

Billy Collins is a popular contemporary poet, which seems like a good thing, but is considered a criticism by some. In the poem below, Collins presents a lovely and sensual extended metaphor for the belief that all genuine poetry, regardless of its anthologized respectability, is the very real and timeless expression of a living human heart.

Taking Off Emily Dickinson's Clothes

First, her tippet made of tulle,
easily lifted off her shoulders and laid
on the back of a wooden chair.

And her bonnet,
the bow undone with a light forward pull.

Then the long white dress, a more
complicated matter with mother-of-pearl
buttons down the back,
so tiny and numerous that it takes forever
before my hands can part the fabric,
like a swimmer's dividing water,
and slip inside.

You will want to know
that she was standing
by an open window in an upstairs bedroom,
motionless, a little wide-eyed,
looking out at the orchard below,
the white dress puddled at her feet
on the wide-board, hardwood floor.

The complexity of women's undergarments
in nineteenth-century America
is not to be waved off,
and I proceeded like a polar explorer
through clips, clasps, and moorings,
catches, straps, and whalebone stays,
sailing toward the iceberg of her nakedness.

Later, I wrote in a notebook
it was like riding a swan into the night,
but, of course, I cannot tell you everything—
the way she closed her eyes to the orchard,
how her hair tumbled free of its pins,
how there were sudden dashes
whenever we spoke.

What I can tell you is
it was terribly quiet in Amherst
that Sabbath afternoon,
nothing but a carriage passing the house,
a fly buzzing in a windowpane.

So I could plainly hear her inhale
when I undid the very top
hook-and-eye fastener of her corset

and I could hear her sigh when finally it was unloosed,
the way some readers sigh when they realize
that Hope has feathers,
that reason is a plank,
that life is a loaded gun
that looks right at you with a yellow eye.

PERMISSIONS